PROPORTIONAL REPRESENTATION

New Electoral System: Proportional Representation
of the majority and the minorities

J. Borély

Translator: Cacildo Marques

Cover picture: Cacildo Marques

Episteme-Ed-Butantan

Copyright © 2017 J. Borély – Translated by Cacildo Marques

All rights reserved.

ISBN: **978-1542339902**

"In a truly egalitarian democracy, every party, whatever it may be, will be represented in a proportion, not superior, but identical, to what it is. A majority of voters should always have a majority of representatives; but a minority of voters should always have a minority of representatives."

John Stuart Mill

Translating: Cacildo Marques, from:

Nouveau Système Électoral:

Représentation Proportionelle de la majorité e des minorités

Par J. Borély

Paris

GERMER BAILLIÈRE, LIBRAIRE-ÉDITEUR

rue de l'École-de-Médecine, 17

M DCCC LXX

CONTENTS

	Introduction	i
1	**1st Part - State of the Question**	Pg 1
2	**2nd Part - Exposition of the System**	Pg 22
3	**3rd Part - Comments**	Pg 40
4	**Post Scriptum**	Pg 70
5	**Translator's Note**	Pg 75

INTRODUCTION

The renewal of the Legislative Body has focused its attention on our electoral system, and particularly on the ever-pending issue of *minority representation*.

The leonine part of the power in the direction of the universal suffrage; the opposition of the cities, annihilated by the adhesion, maybe unconscious, of the campaigns; the electoral circumscriptions already skillfully cut, after being put into order in a second edition expurgated and corrected; the number of official candidates elect, without proportion to the whole scrutiny: all these facts have produced in the country a legitimate emotion, although the spectacle was not unexpected and nothing contrary to the strictest legality - in the vision, at least, of the Legislative Body.

In the circumscriptions where the struggle was intense, the candidates won by a small majority; a few votes decided on the election: 550 in the Calvados, 310 in the Drôme, 3 in the Haute-Saône! Three more voices, there was balance! One vote still, and this vote - or that elector - would nave named a deputy.

Here are 21,000 voters, all electors, all equal in law before the ballot; but, after finishing the counting of the votes, the bureau declared that it had found in the electoral box:

    10,501 ballots expressing a sovereign will, and
    10,499 rags of paper with no value.

This strange accounting profoundly irritates those who are the victims; the most audacious protest in the ordinary form: they sing a little The Marseillaise, break a few street lamps, and go to sleep in prison. Nevertheless, dejection and resignation follow closely; the empire of habits is such that one can persuade oneself, without too much difficulty, that, after all, it cannot be otherwise. The majority is, in short, the majority! The instrument - a scale - is the same for all: one can put suspicion on the instrument provided by the State and pointed out by the State, one can discuss the scale; but one must admit, if not absolute justice, at least the necessity of weighing.

The law of number is only a softened variety of the right of the strongest; attenuation in form, and more apparent than real: nevertheless this law bears the label of civilization, and, as rude as it may appear, it is wise to respect it.

There is confusion here.

The science of numbers is not questioned; arithmetic has no weaknesses, but the different applications that are made of it require different calculations; now, for the electoral operations, the *rule* is not found.

The legal rule is false; I have proved it by some examples; it is good to multiply them.

A number of 120 voters have to nominate 12 delegates: if the meeting contains 30 dissatisfied, or 40 or 50, the delegation should express either a quarter of discontent, one third, or almost half, that is, have in its breast 3, 4 or 5 opponents, as the case may be. Nevertheless, whatever the case, the current mode of voting removes this protest and declares all of them satisfied.

The mode of operation is very simple: one counts the voices, both for this one and for that one; two additions are made, but only one is kept, that which has the highest total; as for the other, it had its reason for being for a moment only to establish the difference.

This meeting of 160 people, it will be France, if you will: instead of 160 voters, we will count 8 million; without a territorial division, the whole country is called like for a plebiscite.

Two lists are in attendance, that of the official candidates and that of the candidates of the opposition, each with 292 names, number of deputies to be elected.

France, forming only one electoral college, but divided in its tendencies, shares its votes unequally.

One knows that 4,400,000 votes are given to the official list, 3,600,000 votes to the list of opposition. What is the result of the ballot? There were 292 deputies to be elected, 292 official deputies are elected.

Thus, 4,400,000 voters are represented, 3,600,000 ballots are thrown into the basket!

Here is the law of the majority as it is understood, here is the legal rule.

Posited in this manner, alone, isolated, and prominent, it would have rose too sharp claims; electoral circumscriptions were imagined:

the operation condemned by 292 similar operations was replaced; one was saved by quantity.

The relative advantage of this measure is understood: the sacrificed minorities do not always sustain the same opinion; not being able to be distributed fairly, it is necessary compensated. But the compensation is quite random; we shall see later how much it is worth.

The rule of double addition is false, this acquired point sufficing for the moment; it is necessary to find another - a rule of proportion.

Now, whatever may be the success of the research, and even that the exact representation of the minorities will be assured, since the law of number does not allow the minority to do to prevail its most legitimate grievances, since the ballot condemns it to vain protestations, what is the advantage of the presence of minorities in deliberative assemblies?

That is because the minority *only* claims the right.

It is not *a party* that I defend, let alone *a party* that I attack: it is a well-known law that I recall.

The minority watches, it keeps the principles, it controls the expenses; despite inevitable exaggerations, it is economical, it is scrupulous, it is just, and it is all this because it is the minority.

The majority is intolerant, tyrannical; it votes the budget as it sees fit and adds what it wants in its own way; it makes the laws and adapts them to its use, and it does all this because it has all the power and because it is the majority.

In England and Sweden, Catholics demand freedom of conscience, absolutely like Protestants in France and Spain.

Under the republic - but under the republic only - monarchists fight at extreme ranges for the inalienable rights of the nation, including *appeal* to the *people*.

Under the monarchy, republicans are passionate advocates of liberty; in power, they establish the dictatorship.

The princes who can replace the aura of exile by the crown of the sovereign are like the minorities, they forget them.

It is because the weak one is the interested defender of justice.

The minority, with a solemnity sometimes declamatory, takes refuge in the temple of the law, which it declares inviolable.

The minority must therefore have a forum; its role is different from that of the majority, but it is equally considerable. If it does not direct the movement, it moderates it, it rectifies it by illuminating the march, showing the danger; if it does not always makes the law to triumph, it affirms it, it proclaims it.

This question of the representation of minorities is not new: it has already been brought to the House of Commons of England, to the Parliament of the Colony of Victoria, Australia, to the Constituent Assembly of the State of New York. In Switzerland (1), a society has been formed for the sole purpose of continuing its examination; in France, in England, in America, etc., Statesmen and publicists (2) adhere to the principle, recognize its importance, and solicit an answer. But, instead of an answer, there are twenty, there are one hundred of them; the speeches succeed the speeches, the pamphlets succeed the pamphlets, and, always posed and unresolved, the question remains, like ever, on the order of the day.

I try my turn.

The representative government appears to be the type definitively accepted by modern societies; this is undoubtedly a progression on the institutions that preceded it. The Parliament, in this system, is the mandatory of the nation; it must reproduce, in a just proportion, the aspirations of its people; it is, or ought to be, the exact reduction of the electors who named it.

It is readily compared to a mirror.

That is the principle. Hitherto the fact has not been able to conform itself.

The mirror is imperfect; the nation does not recognize itself in it, its image is distorted.

The frame of the crystal is too narrow, it does not reflect the minorities, and the electing body, mutilated, loses its proportions and its physiognomy. To enlarge the crystal, to product an irreproachable purity, this is the *desideratum* of the political science.

Mr. Stuart-Mill expressed it perfectly:

"In a truly equal democracy", he says (3), "any party, whatever it may be, would be represented in a proportion not superior to, but identical with, what it is. A majority of voters should always have a majority of representatives, but a minority of voters should always have a minority of representatives. Man to man, the minority should be represented as fully as the majority."

The question is therefore:

How to ensure the representation of minorities?

The debate, as I have said, has been open for so long, the question has been so often and so clearly stated, that I may, without too much inconvenience, remove all preliminary considerations and place *my* answer below of the demand.

But, in my opinion, it is not enough to introduce the minorities into the Parliament: it is still necessary, for making the Parliament to be the sincere representation of the country:

1. To make the coalition of parties impossible.
2. To nullify the dictatorship of the electoral committees;
3. To substitute the freedom of the vote by the discipline.

This is the indispensable complement to the problem.

To discover the formula, the *rule* that guarantees the right of the minorities, is one of the conditions, the first, no doubt, but the others have their importance.

A Parliament *nominated out of the coalitions and committees, by the free initiative of the electors, in which the parties find themselves represented in a proportion not superior, but identical, to what they are, man for man*, will translate *only* in fact what is today just a metaphor, and will be in reality the MIRROR OF THE NATION.

I have seen first how, under the existing laws or the systems already proposed, coalitions are dangerous and nevertheless inevitable, how the role of the committees is excessive and nevertheless legitimate, how the servitude of the elector is humiliating and nevertheless obligatory.

This examination will be made rapidly, summarily; it will assume the reader informed of the discussion; it will be like an immediate continuation of this discussion, like a further investigation, a need for the clarity of a demonstration, sometimes a side of the question to light more vividly: nothing more.

I therefore have the intention - it will probably be read, the pretension - of giving this great question of the right of the minorities a rational solution, hitherto vainly attained.

Two words to justify me, because what I have written is more exact than what one would like to read. Yes, the question posed is a sort of enigma, before which the most valiant and the most illustrious ones have failed; and, without being as perilous as what we have attributed to the fabulous monster of Thebes, it nevertheless preserves for *the unknown* the terrible alternative: guessing or dying, - since ridicule kills. Wishing to play the role of Oedipus on this occasion seems to be rather presumptuous; but here is my excuse:

The solution of the problem, taken in its entire rigor, requires neither science, nor calculation, nor subtlety; the merit is null and void; for this solution is of such simplicity that it has escaped those who preceded me... by its very simplicity!

(1) Reformist Association of Geneva.

(2) Mr. Stuart-Mill, Mr. Thomas Hare, Lord Cairns, Mr. Fawcet, Mr. L. Blanc. Mr. Ed. Laboulaye, Mr. Prevost-Paradol, Mr. Em. de Girardin, etc., etc. (I quote at random a few names among a thousand).

(3) *Representative Government.*

FIRST PART

STATE OF THE QUESTION

I

I leave, without examining its origin and value, the democratic torrent that, under the name of universal suffrage, rumbles as a threat and seems to lead people, who enter there voluntarily or pushed by the governments (and I incline to this last version). The popular waves of electors have invaded England, have flooded France: without a probable dam, they will pour over all Europe.

The universal suffrage is, moreover, a matter of opportunity, not of principle; every people must possess it in its own time. A statistical map of the instruction would suitably rank the nations from the point of view of political rights. This map was made for Europe, not for that purpose; but the brown color, which had fallen to France, would not theoretically be worth, I regret to testify, the price of the capacity that was delivered to it from the enthusiasm of 1848.

According to those ones who are named by the universal suffrage or by the restricted suffrage, the elective assemblies are of a more democratic or more conservative character; but the pending question does not change, the minorities are always inexorably excluded.

This exclusion can take considerable proportions.

"Let us suppose", Stuart Mill says, "that in a country governed by the universal suffrage there is a contested election in each electoral college, and that in every election a small majority wins: the Parliament so formed represents a little more than the simple majority of the nation".

Is it the simple majority? Not even. The electors who compose it, under the yoke of committees, would not be able to arrive at a necessary agreement except by compromises that alter the meaning of the vote and even distort it. We are therefore dealing only with a majority of the majority, or, what is worse and more frequent, with the minority of the majority, when the latter, passive, almost indifferent, allows the imposition of a candidate.

Thus this state of things is possible: a nation, for example, with a liberal majority, and a parliament entirely retrograde; a nation divided, but largely unconcerned, and a Parliament unanimously satisfied; and this Parliament, mandatory of the universal suffrage, saying, too, without being disturbed by reminiscence: *The State is me*!

No doubt, a similar hypothesis would be difficultly realized. A party defeated, in an electoral college, by a hundred votes, can triumph elsewhere by a hundred votes as well; the multiplicity of electoral colleges equals in part the chances, and of all these combined injustices perhaps a general result appears.

Does it suffice for any government to have consulted the nation, and obtained a majority perhaps real? Obviously no.

Let us see! A big question is at stake: the trade treaty with England, the war with Germany, the intervention in Rome, whatever one wants. The Legislative Body, after a passionate debate, formulates a vow, votes an agenda; the famous *never* of Mr. Rouher, for example.

If the Legislative Body represents the nation exactly, the conduct to be kept is very simple: France is, above all, Catholic; our soldiers must keep Rome.

But if the deputies (is it necessary to state that this supposition is purely gratuitous?), if the deputies are the product of an artificial combination; if the administrative pressure, if the suppression of the minorities, if different causes have altered the electoral manifestations; if France is above all liberal; less than that, if there is only doubt, doubt for the government, doubt for the country, what light does bring the *almost* escorted of the equivocal *perhaps*?

Thus the consequence of this situation is strange. There is the known opinion of the House and the presumed opinion of the country; it is not always the same thing. One does not know anything about that. In the sitting that serves me as an example, the minister accentuated the almost unanimous wish of the House; the House applauded the minister. Everything was explained, arranged, agreed upon; an infamy undermost minority protested... And nevertheless the *never*, which seemed an answer, is always *a question*!

If the majority does not have to take into account the pretensions of an insignificant group, lost in the Legislative Body and in the nation, it has the duty to listen to a minority that it supposes numerous. To listen to it is to be ready to make concessions to it; only, in order for these concessions to be made, it is necessary that the majority and the minority no longer question their preponderances, the numerical inferiority of the other, both having their real importance: it is necessary that these qualifications of majority and minority, always contested, are defined by unquestionable ciphers and summarized in a total.

But this total will be obtained only when each *unit* will have a normal value, that is to say, when each deputy will represent an equal number of voters, and when all voters will be represented.

II

The vices inherent to the electoral machine, once reported, the manufacturers begin to work, mainly in England and France. Many projects, some very remarkable, have been presented. Until now, however, the conditions of the specifications have not been strictly fulfilled.

I do not have to examine these projects, even summarily; others have already made it, and better than I could. Each inventor, as it happens, gives the list, provides the inventory and points out the non-values, which includes everything that was proposed before him. I shall deal only with the real assets, that is, with the two least imperfect apparatuses, both of English origin: one theoretically known, the other already operating.

System of Mr. Hare (1)

This system was favorably received by a considerable number of eminent publicists, simplified by Mr. Fawcet (2), modified by the Reformist Association of Geneva, and finally adopted by Mr. Stuart Mil, who ranges "this plan as one of the greatest advances made so far in the theory and in the practice of government", deserves, to all the titles, a special examination.

I borrow the description from Mr. Stuart Mill:

"Under this plan, the representative unit, that is to say, the proportion of voters with right to a representative will be determined by the ordinary method used to obtain the average, the number of voters being divided by the number of seats in the House. Any candidate obtaining this proportion will be elected representative, although this quota consists of votes scattered here and there in a large number of electoral colleges. The votes will, as now, be given locally; but every elector will be free to vote for any candidate in any part of the country in which this candidate has been presented. Thus voters who do not wish to be represented by any of the local candidates can help with their vote the appointing of the person who best suits them among all those who have been placed in the ranks in the whole country. In this way one will give reality to the electoral rights of the minority, which in the other way is virtually deprived of it; but it is important that not only those who refuse to vote for local candidates, but also those who vote for them and who are beaten, may find elsewhere the representation they have not got to obtain in their own district. That is why it was thought to put to each voter a list of voting containing several names, among them that of his favorite candidate. The vote of one voter only serves to one candidate; but if the object of his first choice failed in his candidacy because he had not obtained the proportion, the following perhaps will be happier.

"The voter could put on the list a larger number of names in the order of his preference; in such a way that if the names at the top of his list do not obtain the proportion or obtain it without his vote, the vote may nevertheless be used for the benefit of someone whose appointment will be assisted. In order to obtain the number of members desired to complete the House, and also in order to prevent very popular candidates from absorbing almost all the votes, for a certain number of votes that a candidate can obtain, one counts to him no more than the quota required for his appointment; the other electors who would have voted for him see their votes counted for the first person who, on their respective lists, needs it, and who can, with this help, supplement his proportion.

"In order to determine, among all votes obtained by a candidate, which will be employed at his nomination and which will be given to others, several methods have been proposed, of which we shall not speak here. Naturally, a candidate will guard the votes of all those who would not wish to be represented by another, and, for the rest, to draw lots will be a very passable expedient, if not the best.

"The voting lists will be handed over to a central office, where the votes will be counted, then scored, prioritized by first, second, third, etc.; the proportion will be allocated to the candidates who can perform it, until the House is complete, the first votes being preferred to the second ones, the second to the third, and so on. The voting lists and all the elements of the calculation will be placed in public deposits and accessible to all interested persons, and, if any one, having obtained the required proportion, had not been appointed, as was his right, it will be easy for him to prove it."

Despite the clarity of the exhibition, what is striking first in this system is its excessive complication. In this to-and-fro of bulletins and figures, there is only one candidate who has been ousted, that is to say, a man who is personally interested, who can lose a very long time to control an operation that will remain mysterious to the country.

This machine of bulletins, with its numerous gears, these lists passing through an endless stream, that endless drawing, that frightening pile of useless names surpassing the legal cipher and which must be sacrificed, that bulletin descending from candidate to candidate, and at each time one name decapitated up to what he finds a combination of which he can enter; all this lacks at the primary condition: simplicity, clarity, public control. - The counting of the ballot must give, without effort and with evidence, the result of the struggle.

I do not know if, at the moment when I write, one has found the method to limit and reduce to the elective proportion the number of votes obtained by a candidate; because to draw the luck - I beg pardon of Mr. Stuart Mill - is not even a passable expedient; but the serious defect of this system, a defect which remains, despite the ingenious advocacy of its defender, is to allow parliamentary access only to notables.

The difficulty is already very great, under the present regime, to induce the electors to accept a man of incontestable merit, but placed too close to them, that is to say, inhabiting the same city, the same county, the same department. - Contrary to the laws of optics, the distance increases the candidate.

The elector may bring a local candidate; this name, I am willing it, will be the first subscript on his list; but the second will surely designate the illustrious man whose book or speech sums up his opinion in the most brilliant manner - a celebrity. - The list of preference will be, from this second name, a sort of descendant game, each note of which will express an admiration plus and plus feeble.

It is easy to foresee the results of this method of voting - speakers, historians, poets, novelists, etc., those who carry the sword, especially those who hold the pen, will invade the Parliament, transformed in gallery of great men.

As for the local preferences, incapable of grouping and weakened by the dispersion, they will not succeed. Unless they employ the methods already condemned, the electoral leagues, the committees; unless they appeal to discipline and rebuild what has just been reversed.

I understand, at the rigor, the French Senate so formed - and still can find better! - But I cannot see there the special envoys of the country, the politicians representing the parties and the various interests. The local element being absent, this Assembly will not reproduce the temper, the will, the energy, the rush of the electoral body: babbler, brilliant, learned, wise, literary, it would be an Academy rather than a Parliament.

(1) Tract on the election of representatives
(2) Mr. Hare's Reform Bill simplified and explained.

III

The new system, of which the English constitution has just been enriched, is recommended, on the contrary, by its simplicity.

In every electoral college appointing three deputies, each elector has only two votes.

And that's all.

So, provided that the minority is clever *and disciplined* and joints one third of the voters, it can obtain the nomination of a candidate.

Unfortunately, this is just a partial reform, applying only to towns or counties having 3, 6 or 9 deputies to be elected; because the share of the minority is always the same: a third, whatever its importance.

Mr. James Gortz has developed and perfected this idea, which enables the system to be applied to all electoral colleges. Each elector will have as many votes as there will be deputies to be elected in his circumscription, and will be free to unite, as he sees fit, one or more names.

This plan, Mr. Stuart Mill says, though certainly better than nothing, is only a second-best.

Mr. Prevost-Paradol declares, on the contrary, that it satisfies not only justice, like also reason and the public interest (1). This satisfaction will exceed the measure, once it added a little farther on that this system is closer than any other to exact justice.

Less disdainful than Mr. Stuart Mill, and less enthusiastic than Mr. Prevost-Paradol, I recognize that the system of *accumulated votes* is a happy alleviation of the excessive right of the minorities; - I am not going beyond that.

The weapon placed in the hands of the minorities will be difficult to handle. - In what proportions will the voter distribute his votes?

Who will count before the ballot? The committee, probably. - Where to find the elements of the calculation? In the last vote? However, between two moments perhaps distant, there are so many new events and voters!

It is in these unfavorable conditions that a committee should function! One of the terms of the division will be lacking, and the quotient will be disengaged! It will demand from the electors blind obedience, the only guarantee of success, and the ballot, that *proof* which will come too late, will perhaps declare an operation impossible to rectify.

A double example: there are in a circumscription six deputies to be appointed; the liberal committee believes that it will only get 2. It groups the votes on two names: the scrutinized ballot demonstrates that it will be able to get 3. Let us reverse the proposition: it has ruled that it will have 3; and scattering the votes on three names, no one has emerged victorious. In both cases, as a result of an erroneous estimation, in the loss of one or more appointments, the right of the minority was sacrificed.

The success will then depend, less on the number, on the real strength of a party, than on its skill, or rather, on the chance, of having realized its predictions. The electoral ballot box will be converted into a box surprise.

Without the previous scrutiny (who would dare to ask for such a simple, so rational measure?), there would be a game won by a die roll.

These reservations made, it is certain that, in many cases, this system of *accumulated votes* would have a great advantage over the present system; if not better, as Mr. Stuart Mill says, it would be a very desirable expedient.

As long as the minorities will be not fully represented, as long as a small group of delegates without a warrant will distribute the nominations sovereignly, as long as the voters will obey the committees, as long as the staff, no matter how numerous it is, of the public or private meetings will not have to take into account the absentees, as long as the freedom of the vote will not be substituted for the discipline, there will be justice, reason, public interest, as well as the horizon, *which can be approached as well*, but that moves away from the measure.

(1) New France

IV

Although the electoral system I propose to set out is of general interest and applicable in all countries, I shall not take the reader from the English Parliament to the Spanish Courts, from the Prussian Reichstag to the Austrian Keichsrath. Instead of fatiguing him by making him travel, without great necessity, from London to Madrid and from Berlin to Vienna, it is simpler to choose a nation as a study and stick to it. Since we are in France, let us remain there. It is in this environment, more familiar to the reader, that I shall take my examples, and it is also in France that I shall suppose the realization of the new system.

If it is true, it matters little whether it is dressed in the French style: it will make his way. In passing the frontiers, it will change only in costume and name, and, regardless of its origin, it will be adopted by the nationalities where it will be introduced.

With this explanation made, let us examine the two cogs, both vicious and necessary, which operate in all systems and alter the sincerity of the elections: coalitions and committees.

Let us first look at the coalitions.

They naturally have their partisans and their opponents, and the same men, depending on whether they are in power or opposition, are, one after other, opponents and partisans of the coalitions; one after other, they accuse and excuse themselves. In my opinion, partisans and adherents are equally wrong or equally right.

Doubtless it is strange to see, under a veiled flag, legitimists and republicans, clerical and free thinkers, soldiers so diverse in appearance, silently marching side by side, united by a common hatred. - Thus victory is never more than a truce, for its immediate effect are the disorganization of the triumphant coalition and the formation of a new coalition.

It is therefore a struggle without aim, without mercy, a fight without end, among three parties, of which two, whatever they are, are always leagued against the third, whatever it is!

From this point of view, the coalition is immoral, dangerous, and must be repulsed by honest men. In the political dictionary, the qualification of honest men is employed by the men of a party to designate the adherents of that same party. This means, one by the other, a monarchist, a liberal, a republican, etc. The opinion of the one who uses or abuses this term gives the acceptation. - Mine is taken in the dictionary of the Academy.

But the conditions of the struggle are such that the opponents do not have the choice of the means; the absorption of the minorities poses this imperious alternative: or union, that is to say, the success; or the dispersion of forces, that is to say, defeat, eventually.

To be or not to be that is the question. Hamlet, of course, did not think of the electoral question; but he formulated the excuse of the minorities. Thus, although coalitions are dangerous and immoral, they must nevertheless occur: they are in the situation.

They are in the situation; what proves that they are formed, in spite of all repugnance and antipathy!

It is not with gaiety of heart, it is not without internal revolt that one puts, even for a moment, the hand in the hand of an adversary, for one holds this companion in arms as suspicious, and he is only helped to success in anticipation of his approaching fall.

If Catholic voters, in a minority in a college, could nominate a Catholic candidate, they would not think of making up for the Liberal candidate, and the Liberal electors would not act otherwise if the roles were reversed.

What happens, moreover, whenever a party can dispense its auxiliaries?

It rejects the coalition *virtuously*; it does not even want to hear about it; it has its convictions, its principles and its program: a proposal for an alliance is greeted as an insult.

The candidate, carried by two or more parties, confines himself to the equivocal title of independent; he is pleased with the half-day and with the undertones, while the candidate strongly supported by his political coreligionist stresses, underlines, seeks light; he is not only independent, but also and above all Catholic, Democrat or Radical - as the case may be; - he is him, entirely, with his flag unfurled!

So the only effective way to make coalitions impossible is to make possible the election of a Catholic candidate by the Catholics, the election of a democratic candidate by the Democrats, and so on. It is the adoption of a system that allows the Parliament's access to minorities.

The coalition, it is true, driven from the elections, will enter the Legislative Corps. What is the matter? It will necessarily lose its dissolving character; it will be transformed: instead of the coalition, it will be fusion; instead of the passionate alliance to defeat a common enemy, it will be the rational alliance for the success of a common idea.

The deputies appointed by my system, it will be said, will naturally be worth more or less than their predecessors. The question is not there! They will be strictly linked to their electors, by their mandate (as it will be seen from the exposition of the system), and all minorities being represented, the whole of France, consequently imprinting the movement on what some still call the char of the State, will not be overly concerned with the inevitable jolting of the road.

V

Electoral discipline being a *sine qua non* condition for success, the importance and authority of the committees is perfectly justified;

yet this exorbitant power, confined in a rather arbitrary manner to some electors transformed for the occasion into delegates, was rightly considered as a true abdication.

"The universal suffrage", Garnier-Pagès says in his *History of the Revolution of 1848*, "was distorted from the beginning; it falls, in fact, into the hands of the director committees or between those of the authority."

And Lamennais! - The note is more vehement:

"Are you free, or not? Are you men, or not? The first time you exercise your political right, you are assembled of authority, you are put in the hand a list that you have neither discussed nor even read, and you are said, imperatively: Throw it in the ballot box!"

The reproach is deserved; what confuses me is that it is addressed only to the list system.

I have to write one or more names on my ballot, the committee weighs upon my determination, and, if I have only one name to bear, the constraint is much more disagreeable.

With the list system, with nine or ten names, for example, I find a few that I accept completely and, in any case, I am satisfied with the political significance of the whole, what motivates my vote; while with the individual ballot my adhesion is more precise, it is personal; my statement can go far beyond my intent. That deputy, whom I have not been allowed to choose, whom the committee has chosen for me, is converted, whether I want it or not, in absolute, lively expression of my opinion: - he is me!

The disadvantages of voting by ballot list, which I do not deny, brought more accused perhaps than the individual ballot. In both systems one observes the tyranny of the committees, the servitude of the elector, the moral constraint, the absence of liberty, everywhere and always the sacrifice of the minorities.

The committee is not the great culprit; it obeys, by itself, an imperious law, the necessity. Followed by a handful of courageous citizens, it takes away and occupies with authority a position that one does not even dream of disputing. If there must be a direction by the universal suffrage, the committee takes it; but these courageous citizens, as I call them, or those delegates, as they prefer to call themselves, form a vanguard without any appreciable inference, without any serious connection with the electoral army.

And what I say of the committees applies to public or private meetings: those who are appalled with the tumult, those who think that a candidate does not reveal himself in an hour and in a speech, those who defy the training of the word, these ones do not meet; alones, the impatient ones and the *irreconcilables* arrive there in crowds, and only the orators who join the radicalism of ideas with the vehemence of language can occupy the tribune; moderation, even in form, is a title to ostracism. The frame is enlarged; the picture is the same.

Whatever one thinks of our last elections, and without wishing to diminish its scope, the great majority of the country, it must be said, concerns about political position very incidentally, in its lost moments, and exceptionally every six years, at the week before the vote: it is a mistake, unfortunately it is a fact. All, merchants, laborers, capitalists, farmers, etc., are undoubtedly interested in the affairs of the State, though not considering them as their own affairs. They belong to a party; on occasion, they are capable of a commendable effort, of a limited sacrifice; but this confluence is lukewarm, measured, and circumspect. The stamp of the coins struck in 1830 contained its program in two articles, *Liberty, Public Order*, only they were not in the order of their preference.

In this calm mass, the eye in fire, the fiery speech and the political men agitate themselves. These, like the others, are or may be traders, capitalists, etc., but citizens first. Like the others, they have a family, but they prefer humanity to it; like the others, they have a social position, a private interest, a home; but position, family, interests, they are always ready, even unnecessarily, to lay everything on the altar of the Fatherland!

To be sure, I give pride to the boiling soldiers of democracy and legitimacy, of the partisans of free thought and religious orthodoxy, without inquiring whether small calculations, little hatreds, little ambitions, enter the baggage of the army. This critical point of view is pointless for me: it suffices for me to note the existence of these two forces, one active and the other passive, of knowing how they behave at the time of the elections.

The electoral drama, or the electoral comedy - the genres are mingled - has this peculiarity, that it lacks exposure: it begins with intrigue. As for the denouement, it is often unexpected; here is the record:

The place of the action is of little importance; the action is the same everywhere.

Unexpected news is spread out one morning in a town; - put the name you like: the people learn that the day before delegates appointed a committee. General amazement! - Who did appoint these delegates? One looks at oneself with a smile, another wonders. The list of committee members goes from hand to hand. One did not suspect the existence of this one; that one is very different, his nullity is of public notoriety; if the third name is favorably received, the fourth causes a burst of laughter.

This protest of common sense, or this revenge of mockery, gradually became gradual: one becomes accustomed to what appears to be an enormity, and, on the day of the election, one deposits, melancholy, in a box that takes the name of urn, the ballot paper that the committee has circulated! And I do not accuse this state of affairs, I repeat, neither the voters, nor the committees, nor the candidates.

The *moderates*, the *pales* and the *lukewarm, letting do* ("*laissent faire*"), it is natural that the radicals *do it*. Some are never determined to walk; the others are always ready to run. Luck is all for the latter ones; they may fall, but, only so, they can arrive.

However, the success of these enthusiastic candidatures is rather rare, and this is conceivable: in the presence of candidates who are not his own, the great party (here, great does not translate into courageous or magnanimous, meaning merely extensive, vast, numerous), the lukewarm liberal party loses its cohesion: a fraction undergoes the influence of the committees; another, frightened, supports the official candidate; another, still, abstains (1).

The only consequence I want to draw of the foregoing is that the census of the votes does not give, either precisely or by approximation, neither near nor far, the state of the public opinion; and, incidentally, as from all points of view, the independence of the elector, the choice of the candidate, etc., present perfect parity between the list voting and the individual voting

I use list voting; its rehabilitation is, nevertheless, quite disinterested on my part, for in my system the elector keeps his freedom full and entire. I say *full and entire*, and I emphasize it. The role of the committee is singularly diminished; it becomes what it ought to be, a mere office of consultation, nothing more; and the committee confines itself to its modest and legitimate influence, not because it is more enlightened or better chosen, but by the force of circumstances, because the success no longer depends on discipline.

(1) Abstention, in our political struggles, reaches such considerable proportions that it can not be motivated solely by indifference and by prevention (sickness, absence, etc.); it is necessary to add, for the most part, the impossibility of the elector frequently depositing a vote both useful and in conformity with his opinion.

In 1863, the number of registered voters

was.................................... 9,975,615
and that of abstentions,... 2,692,781
i. e., 29%

In 1869 (1st ballot, 24 May),

registered electors............ 10,315,523
abstentions........................ 2,216,958
i. e., 22%

VI

After the introduction of the committees, it is not fair to do comparison among the official candidacies, although these, alien to my subject, cannot in any way be included in the electoral movement.

The misinterpretation of administrative interference in the legitimate work of committees is wrongly assimilated. The committees are more or less regularly elected, as I have said; however, it is not for the government to raise the objection. The right of assembly is accompanied by obligations so numerous, so minute, so delicate and of a so excessive weakness that there is a great risk of neglecting some. The main ones are known: a room that is not suspect, letters of invitation that are not suspect, and especially guests who are not suspects. These precautions being taken, it remains the evaluation by the Commissioner of Police.

Thus, putting the verification of the powers of the committees at a better time, I return to the distinction I was about to make.

Although to a small degree - it is agreed - the committee represents the voters; the administration represents only the government.

Whatever its composition, the committee is obliged, from the point of view of success, to take a little account of the opinion of the circumscription to which it belongs: it makes and repeats its calculations, it establishes the averages. The prefecture has none of these anxieties: without complicating its work with idle questions of principle, it seeks a man - with his administrative lantern. - The man found, it gives him the majority, as it takes from him, if it changes its mind; and that who is rejected, even at the last moment, recognizes his personal insufficiency so well that he does not even have the idea of maintaining his candidacy.

The principles of *self-government* are so contrary to our habits, they have so little penetrated the public mind, that, either discouragement or impotence, we are all easy to accommodate and transact; so I admit - to some extent - pleasant and sponsored candidacies as such; the Restoration and the Government of July had theirs, the Republic had its own. Other are the official candidacies; they have been inaugurated, it is true, as a progress, as a novelty, and it is right to say that they do not ascend to Julius Caesar and Augustus (1).

They are, however, confounded, especially in the discussions in the Legislative Body (where, at each session, the republican circulars are compared with the prefectural recommendations), official candidacies and agreeable candidatures, and no one, as far as I know, has still clearly characterized the radical difference between the two.

The roles are however reversed: - here the electors are the ones who choose the candidate and the administration is that accepts it; there, on the contrary, the candidate is chosen by the administration and accepted by the electors!

It is the reversal of roles and it is also the overthrow of all accepted ideas.

Agreeable candidates, in spite of the support of the administration, maintain, above all, their mandate from the electors; the official candidates, in spite of the voting of the electors, must, above all, their mandate to the administration.

There is nothing more contrary to the loyal practice of the universal suffrage than this arbitrary nomination, nothing more disdainful than this prefectural gesture which points out a man among a thousand, makes a vacuum around him, highlights him and consecrates him candidate!

One could see this:

A candidate without notoriety, strange to the department, unknown in his circumscription and named to an immense majority!

Some writers - in signed articles! - admired this unlimited confidence, this patriotic abdication; for me, the mere enunciation of the fact is the bloodiest criticism of the system.

These artificial candidacies arise in a state of exception, it will be said: these are feats of strength. What does it matter? They do not testify less the muscular power of those who raise so many bulletins, and, if they have been executed for a few, they may have helped the success of all.

Doubtless the official deputies did not alienate their independence; but, for the few supposed to be in a state of exception, the *favor* of the government incontestably *makes their glory and their power come from it*. Or it is enough, however, that a prefect is suspected of explaining, intimacy, like Augustus with Cinna, that the public conscience demands that the official candidates be *abandoned on their own merits*.

The independence and the devotion adjust like the two halves of the same coin, I do not contradict it; and, if this independence were threatened, they would do their best to see to the end, and, to the last, they would be ready to die... officially. Of course; only it is imprudent to have such a high idea of humanity, to believe that heroism is a common virtue; - I understand this common to all parliamentarians.

One cannot escape from this dilemma: either the one chosen by the administration would have been chosen by the electors, and then the official designation has no object; or, without the support of the administration, he would not have been appointed, and then... the system of official candidacies is condemned!

> (1) (Julius Caesar) recommended his protected ones, sending in all the tribes tablets with these few words: "Caesar, dictator, to such a tribe: "I recommend to you so and so that they may hold themselves the dignity of your suffrage." (Suetonius)

VII

I have only to clear two preliminary questions, both closely related to the system I have to set forth: - the *electoral circumscriptions*; this cannot give rise to any discussion: I need not add a single word to what has been said on this subject, and I could have dispensed myself from treating it; - the other, more delicate, is *the role of the parties in elections*.

The decree of 1852 was intended to form groups of about thirty-five thousand voters, entitled to a deputy.

If this division were adopted, it would undoubtedly have been better to preserve as far as possible the old cantonal lines and leave, in any case, to the departmental and cantonal headquarters their legitimate circle of influence. There would have been, by department, three, four, five homogeneous groups, each with its temperament, its opinion and, consequently, its candidate, a true expression of the local majority; - because it seems that, by requesting a collective response to a considerable number of voters, this answer will be all the more accurate as there will be more facility for prior agreement and community of interest.

One has not judged it thus: instead of reuniting, we have quarreled, mingled, mixed; - one has converted urban waves into rural ocean; the main city being a personality often leafy, sometimes hostile, it was divided, and each circumscription took a slice. The justification of this measure has borrowed its forms from the pastoral, - to the immorality of the working-class population, and the vitiated air of the cities; one has put in their place the laughing picture of the campaign, the pure air of the fields, the campestral virtues... and the rural guards. But why to insist? This attack, without a convincing contradiction, is devoid of purpose, and is in no way related to my system, which demands a vote by ballot list, and by that very fact, larger electoral districts.

I do not want to touch incidentally on the subject I am dealing with - decentralization. I nevertheless take advantage from this neighborhood to use an imperial metaphor, asserting, after many others, that decentralization is the basis of the edifice whose freedom must be the crowning achievement.

The administrative division of France has created, by the habit of nearly a century, a sort of departmental life, very insufficient, doubtless, and which will be weakening; but, in the end, the department is no longer an artificial agglomeration, it is the small country within the great. If the interests of a department are not absolutely distinct from those of the neighbor departments, they are not absolutely the same: the reports are more frequent, the profits are known; and, on the great days of the elections, the desires and hopes of this agglomeration get attached to the delimitation of the administrative boundaries; - other preoccupations, other desires, move beyond. The departmental electoral college unit therefore seems to me one of the good conditions for the equity of elections: - the limits are precise, undisputed; they do not lend themselves to artificial combinations, arbitrary rearrangements; it has a complete, living, independent individuality, which, loyally questioned, can answer seriously.

Voting by department and by ballot list is necessary for the working of my system.

VIII

Although the parties in the governmental spheres do not enjoy a good reputation, and the word, preceded by adjective, becomes the formula of contempt - *the old parties* - it is difficult to get an idea of a country where these elements, these forces of society, would not meet.

In France, more than elsewhere, one resists in considering the parties - the old parties - as an abnormal, irregular, irreconcilable fact with public order; the naivety is pushed so far as to postpone the development of liberties, the crowning of the edifice, at the dawn of that day, which ought never to rise, when the French will bow before a new king-sun and will vote as an only elector.

It is true that such a population, patented, perhaps, with the guarantee of the government, marching on the same road, at medium speed, under the will of the official chauffeur, might well have some value as a work of... political art, but the science of mechanics applied to humanity does not seem to me to be encouraged.

Let us leave the workshops of construction and occupy us with living nations. We shall find the various opinions constantly in struggle, a dull or manifest struggle, according to the degree of civil freedoms, some approving the government purely and simply, others accusing its slowness, others wanting to turn it back or, if one likes it, that there is a *conservative* party, framed by the *progressive* party and the *retrograde* party, that is to say, the old parties!

The mind does not conceive of a world, a people, a city or a tribe that are not targeted by the parties - old and new.

We owe respect to the law - *exterior* respect, - nothing more. We are not forbidden to wish for anything better or for anything else, except that to sustain that the present empire is the typical government, the definitive form, the absolute truth. The boldest ones would not dare to answer so firmly.

What! The unity of opinion in political matter! And the inquisition, the torture, the massacres and the bonfires have not been able to establish religious unity!

We are told that the demonstrations of the parties representing the aspirations of a people who sincerely and unreservedly adhere to the established government are perfectly legitimate, and no one thinks of stifling them (sincerely and unreservedly are so much). Our neighbors offer a good example to follow: the opposition in England is merely aristocratic or liberal, while in France it is above all antidynastic; the government does not have to fighting the parties, but the factions; one is not conservative or liberal, a third party or a democrat, but a Orleanist, a republican, and so on. There is therefore a question of public order, this of preventing conspiracies to be organized.

We answer: It is possible that the old parties are composed, in a large part or in whole, of Orleanists and republicans; we do not know anything, neither you do it. It is an assumption that you make: we will grant that it is probable, if you insist on it; in any case, it is only a supposition. Orleanists or liberals, if they conspire, have the conspirators arrested; democrats or republicans, *if they go down the street*, repress the revolt: it is your right, it is your duty. As for the revolt of ideas, you can do nothing about it. As long as the parties remain on the legal ground, as long as the factious side is not raised, your only weapon is the discussion: the intentions escape you; you can no attack them more than defend them; the subject of the debate is elusive; what there are on both sides is nothing but worthless assertions.

You are waiting for the Legitimists and the Orleanists to have disappeared; no doubt, they will disappear... as the league, the sling, the Dantonists, the Girondins, etc., have disappeared. It is a matter of time; but the parties they represent will be reformed with the same tendencies under other denominations; For what you pursue unnecessarily is a way of thinking, a state of the mind, that is to say, a thing that persists and perpetuates itself. Circumstances give parties a borrowing uniform, an accidental cockade. They sometimes adopt a dynasty, sometimes a characteristic word that is engraved in memory; but the dynasty is extinguished, the word loses its imprint, another great man has come, a more fortunate word has replaced the old one, and the parties simply remain; and, in spite of their transformations, they are followed throughout the ages, in all countries, under all names.

I insist on this banal truth: parties have always existed; they exist legitimately, and, it is good to add, legally. I know of only one manner of suppressing the factions, liberty; I know of none to suppress the parties.

So, whether we like it or not, there are always two parties: one in majority, the one represented by the government; the others in minority, having also their function, their reason for being.

It is important to the stability, to the progress of affairs, that one does not misunderstand the importance of minorities, which can conceal their numerical inferiority by a skillful and noisy tactic, which may even be unaware of this inferiority.

It is equally important that the government, whatever it may be, should not misunderstand the value of the adhesions it obtains: the majority that surrounds it must not be a factitious majority; and it should be not contested. The government is not *a party*; it is or ought only to be the representative of the majority.

Let it be well proved to every one that the old parties are in a minority, and the old parties will become modest, and this demonstration will disconcert all the *Orleanist conspiracies*, and it will repress morally, and victoriously, all the *republican insurrections*.

Let it be proved, on the contrary, that the uneasy country, discontented, inclines to the right or the left, and the government, whether willingly or unwillingly, will march in the direction indicated.

In both cases, exact knowledge of the public opinion and, consequently, a binding agreement between the nation and the governments, this can be translated so: *security for the government, tranquility for the nation.*

Thus the existence of the parties and the official recognition of their strength or weakness are the very elements of stability.

I can now approach the exposure of my system.

SECOND PART

EXPOSITION OF THE SYSTEM

IX

The road which we have just traversed, though encumbered with the debris of all systems, vicious gears, straps too stiff, etc., under the names of committees, coalitions, etc.; this road, I say, fatiguing, doubtless, but easy, has led us to the threshold of my studio; in other words, the critical moment has arrived, and the reader awaits of my part my little machine!

I am somewhat disturbed, but by a very different motive: my little machine is so simple that it is inconceivable that it should not have imposed itself, priorly, upon my illustrious predecessors.

It requires neither study nor preliminary work; it adapts to all forms of government; it can work in France, for example, within twenty-four hours; moreover, it abridges the current operations by abolishing the second round of the scrutiny.

So far the problem has been badly posed, and, as a result, there are *the* solutions, instead of the existing *one* solution.

For one to know how to put it, the simplest is to examine how the elector himself poses it; because he posits it, naturally, in an unconscious manner, and, for that reason, perhaps in a more exact manner. So, let us report ourselves to the electoral period.

Each party formulates, I dare not say its principles - since the principles of 89 are invoked by all parties, even by our constitution! – but, let us say, its program. If there is a discussion on this, the party splits and forms two distinct groups. If there is a question of the left, one will continue to call itself *democratic*, the other will take the title of *radical*. Until then, there was no difficulty; the stumbling block is *the choice of the candidate*.

The choice of candidates was a privilege reserved exclusively to the committees and newspapers, or to ones reserved for them. The Law on Public Meetings has modified, at least in Paris, the way of operating. I say in Paris because this law, a sort of liberal flourish, wrapped in the condition of a button in the letter of the 19th of

January, was not able to flourish in the icy atmosphere of the Legislative Body, and the suspicious provincials scarcely appraised it.

The modification, however, is more in form than in substance; the meetings are, all the same, only the branches of the committees; the difference is that one does not deliberate in closed door and the staff is more numerous.

There was no contradiction in the committees; it is suffocated in the meetings: the tendencies and the procedures are the same; a little more people, and that's all. One has only the staff, one has the whole regiment; the bulk of the army is always outside.

The physiognomy of the electoral body, if one may express it thus, is changing; it offers at least three aspects: frontally, it is smiling; seen from the right side, it is anxious, mistrustful even to insult; on the left, it is fierce; it is only the fierce side what one sees in the meetings.

In Paris, the vote of the 24th of May (I deal only with the first vote, the only one with a small extent, but ultimately the only one with a certain significance) demonstrated that the unanimity of opinion in the meetings does not prove even the simple majority in the electoral circumscription.

In the first, Mr. d'Alton-Shee has all the ovations imaginable, and he arrives at the last on the list of voters. In the seventh, Mr. J. Favre cannot even make himself heard, and his name brings the most votes.

And if was this the part of training? If one were to question those who have seen, those who know - Maitre François, for example - they would say to you: "All the others, *crians* and *bellans* in such intonation, began to jest, to jump afterwards to the queue. The crowd went to the first to jump after his companion, etc." (*)

I would deviate from the part I have plotted in pursuing this idea. Let us return to the observation of facts, to the pure and simple observation of the electoral movement.

In the departments, the choice of candidates comes up against other difficulties. Generally there are not three or four indisputable notables: there are indeed a dozen possible candidates, not avowed, indecisive postulants hiding or letting their pretensions; but these ten candidates of various merits are insufficient individually to rally the majority; they are, furthermore, too close to those who owe nominates them; they lack perspective. Between this one here and the other there, the elector, solicited, hesitates: he thinks they are worth, and sometimes even that he deserve them. These ten competitors also hold, it must be confessed, that one of them leaves the ranks; the alignment does not hurt any susceptibility.

If the universal suffrage had to pronounce itself directly, without troubling about the lost votes, it would be distributed on these ten candidates in a very unequal manner. It would indicate the difference that the public opinion puts between them; and he who would find difficulty to organize a committee to sponsor his candidacy would perhaps triumph over the ballot.

In short, or one abstains, because none of the possible candidates, anticipating a deaf hostility, dares to take a step forward; or one votes with no enthusiasm for one of them, and one votes for that one because a fortuitous circumstance has decided so, because he has some devoted friend, perhaps because he is the most mediocre of all; or calls a foreign candidate. If this latter method has the disadvantage of leaving local candidates in the shadows, it also has the advantage of leaving them all in the shadows.

So the candidate is always the obstacle, sometimes, insurmountable obstacle, sometimes turned, sometimes exempted; but he is turned or exempted because one invokes in time a *superior* interest: the honor of the flag, the triumph of the party!

The candidate is what divides; the political flag is what brings together.

The object is the success of an idea, a principle, a party; the candidates are only *the means*.

The goal is unique, of a *superior* interest, as I have said; *the means* are numerous, almost indifferent.

The elector has the choice of means, that is to say, of the candidates; he subordinates him to different considerations: it is a question of tactics, of discipline, of probability, nothing more.

In fact, the things do not happen otherwise.

I still take my example in the Paris elections, and in the circumscription (the second), where each party was represented by one candidate.

All the conservative voters who took part in the election voted for Mr. Devinck. Does this mean that Mr. Devinck was their man to the exclusion of all others? - Did those who met under the name of Mr. Thiers consider Mr. Thiers the only representative able to represent them? - Did those who give their vote to. Mr. d'Alton-Shee would not have been indifferent to Mr. Gambetta or Mr. Rochefort? It cannot be denied. Perhaps some of those who voted for Mr. Devinck preferred Mr. Granier de Cassagnac (this hypothesis does not imply any preference on my part); perhaps also the electors of Mr. d'Alton-Shee would have gladly passed over to Mr. Cantagrel; but all of them, regardless of their inclination, voted or for the official candidate, or for the candidate of the third party, or for the radical party, because they were themselves conservatives, third party or radicals - *and only that.*

Thus, so far, the problem has been misplaced.

One does not vote *uniquely* for the candidate; one votes for both a candidate and a party.

Or rather:

ONE VOTES FIRST FOR A PARTY, NEXT FOR A CANDIDATE.

My system is entirely contained in the statement of this banal truth.

(*) In Rabelais (TN)

X

We shall see whether, on these new bases, it is difficult to establish a simple, accurate, freely operating electoral machine, and, this time, in keeping with the specifications.

The elector belongs, willingly or unwillingly, to one of the three great parties that divide the citizens of the same country:

Or he is satisfied - pro-government party,

Or he regrets - retrograde party;

Or he hopes better - progressive party.

In France, under the parliamentary system, these parties were known - they still are - under the names of *center, right, left.*

I do not take into account the nuances; this summary division is sufficient at present (1).

This classification, it is not done by me; - it exists naturally, inevitably: *it cannot fail to exist.*

The citizen applying as a candidate also belongs, willingly or unwillingly, just like the voter, to one of these three parties; - only, in my system, he is required to declare it publicly. A candidate is something other than an individuality: he is still and above all a flag, and - in order not to leave room for equivocation - this flag bears the motto: center, right or left, that is to say, a word of which no one is unaware of its meaning.

The elector voting, as has been said, *first* for his party, *then* for various candidates, must also mention on his ballot, *first* his rallying flag, *then* the men to whom he entrusted the defense.

The electoral bulletins would thus have the following aspect:

LEFT WING	CENTER	RIGHT WING
Gambetta, Piccard, E. Picard, etc., etc.	Devinck, Bouley, Denière, etc., etc.	Cochin, De Larcy, Keller, etc., etc.

The voting would take place by department and in the ballot list, each department having a number of deputies proportional to that of registered voters.

This is the new system in all its simplicity!

Let us now enter the central census office.

With the bulletins verified, counted and ranked, the first operation is to find the number of deputies to be allocated to each category.

Two divisions are sufficient to obtain this result.

The total of the votes cast, divided by that of the deputies to elect, gives the votes required for each category for the appointment of *one* deputy.

The total votes of each category, divided by the quotient already found, gives the number of deputies to be allocated to each of them.

I assume 200,000 voters and 8 deputies to be elected, what is to say:

Voters	Deputies to elect	Electoral quotient
200,000	: 8	= 25,000

	Votes obtained	Quotient	Deputies to be allocated to each category	Votes not used
Center	103,300	: 25,000	i.e., 4	+ 3,300
Right	36,200	: 25,000	i.e., 1	+ 1,200
Left	70,500	: 25,000	i.e., 2	+ 20,500
	200,000		7	25,000

These 25,000 votes not used, these *remains* totalized, form the electoral quotient, and, naturally, the party, or the category, which has the most considerable fraction names the complementary deputy (2).

In the above hypothesis, it is therefore appropriate to attribute 4 deputies to *the center*, 1 to *the right* and 3 to *the left*.

According to the order already established, we had to seek:

First, the number of deputies to be attributed to each opinion;

Then, in each opinion, the candidates who were to be appointed deputies.

The first point is made; the three parties: *left, center, right*, have a number of representatives in perfect relation to their importance.

The second, more secondary - I support this subordination, which characterizes my system - presents no difficulty. The candidates nominated in each category are those who have obtained the most votes.

> (1) The subdivision of the parties presents no difficulty, but it might hamper here the clarity of the exposition.
>
> (2) This operation is, basically, only one rule of three; it nevertheless differs from it by the question of the *remains*, which here express only a proportion, of the proportional fractions, while in the double division they represent exactly the unused votes.

XI

Let us apply to the elections of 1869 this operation, as simple as it is correct.

This work will not be complete, in the sense that the classification of votes into three categories is no longer possible; in the sense also that the elector did not vote *freely* neither for his party nor for his candidate: - there was coalition, agreement, compromise.

In Paris, for example, in certain circumscriptions, Catholics, the third party, the left and the radicals voted together, against the official candidate; in others, on the contrary, the conservatives may have voted with the left; in others, finally, the mixture was so confused, the combat was so badly engaged, that they will dispute for a long time on the name of the party then victorious.

When questioned, France, instead of replying, uttered a formidable cry, composed of eight million votes - they were counted; - what did they say? The indications of the ballot are so vague that everyone demands it: the official interpreter asserts that the personal government is fortified by the electoral verdict, while the *left* there found the certainty of its pacific advent, and the party of the *irreconcilables*, the announcement of a forthcoming revolution.

Alas! The country, consulted, *speaks a language* very imperfect, very poor, and which knows its penalty. It stirs, it rolls its menacing eyes; by the energy of the gesture, it hope to supply the impotence of the speech. But it does not understand. How to understand? Words are lacking, definitions too.

It is the dictionary that will provide the new system.

I shall, therefore, confine myself, as it stands, to the only apparent divisions: the *official* candidates and the candidates of the *opposition*, and still - especially for Paris - the line separating the two camps is indecisive. If, on the one hand, there are the *legitimists*, the *Catholics*, the *irreconcilables*, the *left*, the *third party*; on the other hand, there are the *official* candidates, the *doubtful* candidates, the *pleasant* candidates and even the *unpleasant* candidates, but imposed by the circumstances. Between these and the third party, how to distinguish? What places will we assign to Mr. Olivier and Mr. Cochin? If I put them in the official list, they protest. If I mix them with the opponents, I no longer find them in the circumscriptions where they have taken the governmental votes! What to do? It is a vice inherent in the system that takes to one sole basis the candidate; when the candidate is discussed, he is alternately claimed and rejected by all parties.

I will therefore employ, for Paris, more vague denominations, so as not to reveal any susceptibility; but this classification of the candidates does not matter, it does not affect the straightness of the operation, and the question is all there. We deal with the representation of the *parties*; so much the worse for the candidate, whose opinion is a subject of discussion.

ELECTIONS OF PARIS (23rd and 24th May, 1869)
Voters....................314,435
Abstentions..............85,977
Registered................400,412
9 deputies to elect.
The more or less pleasant candidates had..........................75,429 votes.
The candidates of opposition...239,006 votes.

On this data, we will operate as it was already said:
The total of the votes cast, divided by that of the deputies to be elected, gives the electoral quotient. Thus:

Votes expressed	Deputy to elect	Electoral quotient
314,435	:9	= 34,937

Therefore, 34,937 votes are necessary for the appointment of *one* deputy.

The total votes of each category, divided by the quotient already found, gives the number of deputies to be allocated to each. Thus:

	Votes	Electoral quotient	Deputies	Votes
M or L agreeable	75,429	:34,937	=2	+ 5,555
Opposition	239,006	:34,937	=6	+29,384

Result (1)
2 deputies More or Less agreeable
6 deputies of opposition
1 deputy of opposition (complementary)

The first operation is completed: each group of 34,937 voters entitled to one deputy, the opposition has 7, the government 2. The majority is only the majority; it has not increased at the expense of the minority; both are what they ought to be.

The second operation is simpler. To appoint the elected

representatives, it is sufficient to classify the candidates in the order of the votes obtained, by drawing up two lists, since here we have only two categories.

Candidates more or less agreeable	Votes	Opposition	Votes
E. OLLIVIER	12,848	J. SIMON	30,350
COCHIN	12,478	E. PICARD	24,444
DEVINCK	10,404	PELLETAN	23,410
BOULEY	9,810	BANCEL	22,848
LACHAUD	8,742	GAMBETTA	21,744
DENIÈRE	7,229	RASPAIL	14,470
LEVI	7,054	GARNIER-PAGÉS	14,346
Diverse	..6,864	Diverse	.87,394
	75,429		239,006

The first two on the official list and the first seven on the opposition list would be proclaimed deputies (2).

This table of candidates has, under present conditions, no significance: as much as J. Simon is the first, Raspail the sixth, although J. Favre is the last, lost in the *Diverse*, it is not an argument so that the public opinion put J. Favre below Raspail and J. Simon above all of them. No! The existence or absence of rival nominations, the circumstances under which these applications have happened, the accidental causes of agreement or disagreement do not surpassing the boundaries, etc., have increased or decreased the number of votes obtained and have removed any value from this numerical ranking.

The new system - as we have undoubtedly noticed - frustrates all intrigues and renders illusory the abusive interference of the committees. The electoral ballot has two distinct parts, the elector emits at the same time two votes: the first, *obliged*, for his party; the second, *free*, for his candidates. The first ensures the triumph of his opinion, the second is only the manifestation of a personal preference. The vote for the candidate is a testimony of esteem, of consideration, and, consequently, the seats occupied at the top of the summary table are places of honor. This table becomes even a curious thermometer, marking the degrees to where the politicians can be raised, and, in addition, according to the times, the changes of opinion.

So much for Paris. It would not be without interest to repeat this same operation for some departments, notably the Rhone, the Gironde, the Bouches-du-Rhone. I confine myself, however, to the Gard, which I choose for the singularity of the result.

ELECTIONS OF THE GARD

			Votes for the candidates	
Circumscription	Registered	Voters	Officials	Opponents
1st	35,216	25,939	11,465	14,474
2nd	30,801	7,953	21,472	13,519
3rd	41 001	28,776	16,702	12,074
4th	25,838	21,193	11,824	9,369
	132,856	97,380	47,944	49,436

It is easy to see that, if the department was bowled by a prefectural embargo, the divisions adopted disconcert habits and offend common sense, whereas the city of Nimes is cut into three pieces skillful related to the circumscriptions that surround it, this upheaval did not excuse the need to form electoral groups of equal importance, since a circumscription only has 25,838 voters, while another has 41,001(!).

Despite the difficulties accumulated on the field of maneuver - it is not to read maneuvers - the opposition, as one sees, holds firm before the official candidates; the forces are almost equal on both sides.

The regulation I am about to make falls in such a way to the sense that it is already made in the mind of the reader.

Voters	Deputies to elect	Quotient
97,380	:4	= 24,145

What is to say, 2 deputies for the government and 2 for the opposition.

I complete by the two lists of candidates.

Officials	Votes	Opposition	Votes
DUMAS	16,702	TEULON	10,609
ANDRÉ	11,824	CAZOT	10,515
TALABOT	11,465	PASQUET	4,912
GENTON	7,953	DE CRUSSOL	4,137
		Diverse	19,966
	47,944		49,436

The first two on the official list and the first two on the opposition list will be proclaimed deputies.

That is not how it happened. In the *Seine*, by the present system, *all* the candidates of the opposition have triumphed; there were, however, a minority of 75,429 voters who are not represented.

In the *Gard*, the contrary is true: *all* the official candidates have been appointed. There was, however, not even a minority, but, thanks to the clever division of the circumscriptions, a majority of 49,436 voters that are not represented.

And these voters, in considerable number, repulsed, sidelined, scratched in fact from the lists of electors, find themselves in all the points of France. Multiply these minorities sacrificed by the districts - deducting a few *rotten boroughs* - and you will admit that half the country has no representatives! It has been pretended that these vices of *detail* are attenuated mutually by their contrary results, that the operation must be judged from above and taken as a whole. The inevitable compensations should restore, if not in their integrity, at least to a great extent, the respective strengths of the various opinions, and this should result in a very acceptable average.

PROPORTIONAL REPRESENTATION

We will show, by the table of general elections in 1863 and 1869, that these conjectures are worth.

GENERAL ELECTIONS
1863

Voters	Deputies to elect	Quotient
7,214,292	:283	= 25,492

	Votes	Quotient	Deputies
Officials	5,354,779	: 25,492	i. e., 210
Opposition	1,859,513	: 25,492	i. e., 73

Therefore:

	Officials	Opposition
Mathematical result	210	73
Legal result	250	33

For 1869, it is on the record of the votes given by the newspaper *La France* that I will operate. I cannot control it and do not want to challenge it; but its semi-official origin suggests that it is not unfavorable to the government.

GENERAL ELECTIONS
1869

Voters	Deputies to elect	Quotient
8.098.565	: 292	= 27,734

	Votes	Quotient	Deputies	Votes

Not recommended,

Third party........	1,124,598	: 27,734	i. e., 40	+ 15,238
Orleanists, Clericals, etc.....	786,020	: 27,734	i. e., 28	+ 9,468
Democrats not radicals.......	1,507,648	: 27,734	i. e., 54	+ 10,012
Radicals...................	153,263	: 27,734	i. e., 5	+ 14,593
Votes lost.................	71,749		5	
Officials...................	3,643,278	: 27,734	132	
	4,455,287		i. e., 160	+ 17,847
	8,098,565		292	

The votes lost (and my system does not have them) give an additional deputy to each category.

	Officials	Opposition
Mathematical result	160	132
Legal result	92	200

I have just compared two systems, or rather, two rules of arithmetic, what is to say that *everybody can verify*.

One is ill-conceived, ill-posed, ill-resolved: one is *evidently false*, the other is *evidently exact*.

I'll come back here one last time.

When the votes are counted, common sense, justice, arithmetic, tell you at the same time:

In Paris, the majority will have 7 representatives, the minority, 2.

In the Gard, the majority, very weak, should have 2 representatives, the minority, 2, as well.

The *present system* answers:

In Paris, the minority will not be represented; and in the Gard, better still, the majority will not even be represented.

The system of *accumulated votes can* perhaps respond, *approaching justice*. The probable part of the opposition is here, that of the government is there - *roughly*.

As for my system, he will answer as he has answered and as common sense, justice and arithmetic want.

The minority will be represented at Paris, like the majority in the Gard, and (assuming - what is inadmissible - that the new system will not have largely modified the voting of 23 and 24 May) each department provides its share of adhesion and blame, computing for the Legislature 160 official deputies and 132 deputies of the opposition, i. e., for the government a *weak*, but a *true*, majority of 28 votes.

(1) One obtains the same result by the *rule of three*.

Candidates more or less pleasant

Votes cast	Deputies to elect		Votes obtained	Deputies	Fractions
314,435	:9	::	75,429:x	=2	+ 15

Candidates of opposition

| 314,44 | :9 | :: | 239,006 : x | =6 | + 84 |

(2) Comparative table. Elections of 1863.

Voters	Deputies to elect	Electoral quotient
224,036	: 9	= 24,892

	Votes	Quotient	Deputies	Votes
Officials	79,147	: 24,892	=3	+ 4,471
Opposition	144,889	: 24,892	=5	+ 20,429

XII

It is impossible to know what the universal suffrage will give when the *free* voter will be able to, without affecting the success of his party, vote for candidates truly chosen by him; but there is no temerity in asserting that the result will be very different from that which I pointed out on the voting of 1869. In any case, the government, like the opposition, will find useful information there (one can read formation, lessons).

The cipher of 35,000 registered voters for a deputy is too high; a considerable minority will run the risk of disappearing: reduced to 20,000 or 25,000, it will satisfy the most extreme demands.

In the preceding work, I divided the votes into only two categories: government and opposition. That is what one could do; but the theoretical division is quite different, I already have said it, and I must return to this subject.

There are, first of all, three elementary groups: progressive, governmental and conservative or retrograde, i. e.:

Left - Center - Right

This is only a first rank; the parties that draw the government in the opposite direction are formed in such a way that they demand a new division. The groups which it produces have popular denominations that one should preserve, since they indicate a known political program (1).

The series is then completed as follows:

Center
Center Left   *Center Right*
Left   *Right*

At a first glance, it seems that any voter could politically fall into one of these divisions, adopt one of these programs, and that the elections made in these conditions will give a sufficient statistic of opinion.

This, however, is not enough. If the *right* side holds the indicated divisions, the left-hand side requires the extension of the series; after the *third party* there are the *democrats*, and beyond the democrats there are the *radicals*. I do not know whether I should place the irreconcilables higher or farther.

It will therefore be convenient to adopt the following table:

Center
Center Left   *Center Right*
Left   *Right*
Extreme left   *Extreme right* (2).

With this table completed, the prism that shows the seven political colors gives full satisfaction to all opinions, it nevertheless having, in some rare cases, a relative disadvantage by the very dispersion of the votes. The minorities will feel wronged in the departments that will be entitled to a small number of deputies.

Let us admit 60,000 voters, 3 deputies to be elected.

	Votes	Quotient	Deputies	Votes
Center	48,000	: 20,000	i. e., 2	+ 8,000
Left	7,000	: 20,000	i. e., 0	+ 7,000
Extreme left	5,000	: 20,000	i. e., 0	+ 5,000

The center, by its preponderant fractions, will appoint the 3 deputies.

Is it right? I do not believe that; obviously, in this example, the left and the extreme left are subdivisions of the same party, and these 12,000 voters, as the case has been foreseen so much the option has been offered, if they will probably be united, the most weak ones will give up to the stronger ones, rather than letting the government candidate to pass, in other words, the opponent.

I might vary these combinations to the infinite; but it is not necessary: we will always find the fighters probably preferring a half success to a defeat. Is it impossible to take this preference into account? Not at all.

Let the elector be free to confine himself to the exclusive assertion of his party, or, more conciliatory in the anticipation of the failure, let he may add to his bulletin a possible destination, what he will express in a very simple way.

This is the amended bulletin; it differs from the first only by the simple addition of a word, that is to say, of a disposition subordinate to a foreseen case:

LEFT	EXTEME LEFT
-	-
Extreme left	Left
E. Picard,	Gambetta,
Bethmont.,	Raspail,
Carnot,	Esquiros,
etc.	etc.

What I say about the left and the extreme left applies naturally to all parties.

The recapitulation will be done first taking into account only the first indication, and the party which will win the most votes will benefit from those which have been reserved to it, in the absence of useful employment, by the express will of the voters.

And one should not cry out to the coalition! To overthrow the common enemy, one votes *with* the party that attacks it, one does not vote *for* this party; the agreement is generally made on a candidate multicolor, equivocal, erased and sometimes - in desperate cases - on a candidate of color frank, red or black, but then expressly reserving the principles: in my system, *with preferences*, the coalition has not this propitious ground (the candidate), for it is pronounced *on the principles themselves*; one adheres to a precise program, which forbids compromises and tolerates only the association between two neighbor shades, the welding between the juxtaposed parties!

Suppose, now, general elections made under these conditions. To each of these denominations is added a question mark: the questions are these - suppose the answers. Under these seven programs, put numbers - the votes cast - and say if there is room for equivocation; if from the outcome of the ballot the sovereign will of the majority will not emerge clear, indisputable; if all minorities will not be represented; if the set so formed will not be the exact reduction of the electorate!

(1) It is superfluous to point out that these denominations are not, however, compulsory. This is not a necessity of the system, it is my opinion on a detail of execution; only these denominations, in order to preserve their character of *public order*, require a legal sanction. An electoral law must specify and limit them; for if it is indifferent that the parties are designated by the terms Left Center, Left, Extreme Left - or Third Party, Democrats, Radicals, - it is not improbable that they appear under the heading (most often false) of

Legitimists, Republicans, Orleanists, etc.

(2) This table causes an observation. A government representing the average of the public opinion would also be solicited on the contrary by the opposing parties; how is it that the left series (the liberal party) answers exactly and completely to the current struggle of the parties, while one almost does not use the right series? Instead of being at the center, is the government at one of the extremities?

THIRD PART

COMMENTS

XIII

In the first part of this work, I have assisted the reader with a somewhat rapid definition of the pending electoral questions, constantly observing the inconveniences and defects of the solutions given by the current system. These same questions will again pass before our eyes, but applying themselves to the system that I have just described, and of which the superiority is manifested by comparison, will be easy to demonstrate, now that we possess the bases of the discussion.

This definition, like the preceding one, will not detain us beyond measure: long developments, minutious elucidations, ample and bold dissertations do not enter into the plan that I have adopted, and which consists in relying on collaboration of the reader; for there is some presumptuousness in keeping him too long on the same subject, in forcing him to retrace his steps, as if he had forgotten or not understood, to make him weigh one by one all the arguments, doing not spare him a detail or a comment!

I have also to examine carefully, scrupulously, the obstacles, the inconveniences and the perils of the new road that I open to the universal suffrage. I do not, however, pretend to notice everything, to discover everything; perhaps it will happen to me to walk on a stony ground, without declaring it - it is because I am not aware of it; - to pass before a precipice without stopping there, - is that I will not have seen it!

I have already answered the inevitable objection: the alleged danger of party representation. There, I know, tenacious as a prejudice, this will resist front to all arguments, and, twenty times abated, it will always rise with triumphant airs. I should have to point out, without success, that, since there are parties in the country, since they are in the Chamber, since they are in all the assemblies, in the department as in the commune, since there, in the darkness, under the mask, my system, from this point of view, produces no other effect than that of a torch; it will illuminate the danger, if the danger exists. Lost Lyrics! The conservatives, the vigilant guardians of the social order, prefer to look in the night, trembling, these black silhouettes, without knowing exactly what they want and what they can - their audacity goes far! - or they close their eyes, - their prudence goes far!

It must therefore refrain from chasing away the specters of the parties and abandoning these visionaries, all the more so because I hear, although distant, two requests for interpellation: one on *parliamentary* coalitions, the other on the need to *direct* the universal suffrage, and I see, near me, menacing, a triple objection awaiting me - a sharp weapon, with three points, leaving only the choice of the wound.

Let us first hear this:

The table of the parties is incomplete, and, nevertheless, it divides the country into categories too narrow; the precious interests are excluded, sacrificed, and the national assembly is composed of minorities, unimportant and without character. The great parties no longer exist; the universal suffrage, lost in distinctions that escape it, populates the Legislative Body of heterogeneous representatives, incapable of matching and grouping: instead of two flags, seven handlebars!

Let us make a little light around these objections; let us examine them separately.

Is the enumeration of the parties, as I have given it, complete? All political parties, no doubt, are there; however - this is the first objection specified - purely religious, purely local, purely commercial interests, social reforms, do they not also form distinct groups, which should be represented?

All this is still a little confused.

There are the *permanent* interests and the *accidental* interests: the former are always linked to the political parties, the others are usually detached from them.

The *Catholics*, the *socialists*, answer to the permanent interests, and, as such, they make common cause with the political parties; they are confounded with them, they accentuate them; at certain epochs, they exaggerate their significance.

In France, at present, some or many call themselves Catholics and *exclusively* Catholics; but by their doctrines, by their tradition, by their journals, by their candidates, they are truly a political party. It is the party of *authority*, - add monarchy; it is the party of *right*, add the word *divine*, effaced because of unpopularity: it belongs to the *right wing*. In the same way, the Protestant party, if it existed, it would appear on the *left wing*.

The religious interests are thus included in my picture. There is nothing to worry about; nothing would prevent the Catholic party from choosing in the series *right* - where many seats are vacant - a label that would suit it, a conventional etiquette under which it will be united.

As for the socialists, they are divided into two categories: one is accommodated to the personal of the government, the other is welded to the extreme left.

The local and commercial interests are accidental. Let us get rid of the first ones.

These local interests, for respectable they may be, have nothing to do here; first of all, because a deputy is not the special advocate of a circumscription, but the representative of a political party. We must fight against this narrow spirit and not favor it. An assembly composed of equal representatives will be without moral value, without principle; absorbed in the contemplation of the budget, it scarcely will disturb the august sleep of any majesty. - Nothing to do again because the local interest is always defended by the deputy of the locality and attacked by the deputy of the neighbor department, whose interest is contrary. One has only to recall the joyous episodes brought about by these discussions: railway tracks, improvement of navigable ways, entry fees on foreign wines, etc. As soon as the interest of two departments in rivalry is at stake, two scheduled deputies rise at the same time, taking, one after other, the word - to the laughter of the House - and the two orators, a little irritated at first, soon will take part in the general hilarity.

What, in fact, is a representative of the local interest? For the electors, he is a complacent protector; for the administration, he is a protected docile. Or the local interest is legitimate, and the deputies of the department, whoever they are, are the natural defenders; or, as a privilege, it can only be satisfied by a favor: - a favor is granted only in exchange for a service. Or, if the deputy is so thanked by the government, he must, in good morals, when he presents himself before his voters, be thanked otherwise!

The question changes with general interests, in the same purely material order; it may have, at a given moment, an importance, an extreme severity, almost separating the country into two camps: - that of free trade is in this case.

I understand, then, not the necessity of increasing the nomenclature of the parties, leaving the electors free to vote on the political questions or on the economic questions; for this half-party Chamber, representing only arbitrary fractions of opinion, will express only factitious majorities. No, I understand better the convening of special representatives, - a commercial session. - My system will respond perfectly to this need; - the bulletins, instead of having for signs: *left - center - right*, it will carry the required indications, *free exchange - protection*, etc.

A last - and reserved - argument, which excludes the three unrepresented interests at the same time:

Voters are not asked at the same time for *two separate*, unrelated questions, and this for the excellent reason that, being unable to answer to *one only*, they will be forced to opt, to sacrifice that one or that other. The political question takes precedence over all others.

In the last election, *protectionist* candidates were not appointed to the circumscription where their supporters were, however, in the great majority. - The *political* candidate, *exclusively*, was in cause. - It will never be otherwise.

And it is not only on the occasion of the appointment of deputies to the Legislative Body that politics excludes and absorbs the interests which attempt an unequal struggle: it has its obligatory place - the first - in all electoral meetings. With or without profession of faith, and in spite of innumerable denials, the councilors-general, the councilors of county, the councilors of town, etc., are political candidates. The contrary opinion has for it, I do not ignore, almost unanimity: from the extreme right to the extreme left, without the line being broken, without gaps, all parties theoretically call men of good will on this neutralized ground; the law itself comes to their aid and formally banishes politics. However, in reality, - the show is before our eyes every day - these elections have a political character; the general councils issue political vows, the presidents of these councils give political speeches. There are political conflicts between mayors and municipal councils; the district councils make political demonstrations, and the newspapers and the parties record with satisfaction these political victories!

Should we regret this invasion? It is the general opinion, it is the opinion of these sad publicists who persist in the search for new combinations and construct ingenious dykes, which will not prevent the political waves from passing over or crossing; - and I am glad of it, and I add that the constitutional machine needs this driving force.

The political rights, strongly despised by the theorists born of the coup d'etat (governmental school, Émile Ollivier branch), are, without error of forgetting, the guarantee par excellence of public freedoms. These rights, must be affirmed, one must use them in every way, in regard to everything, for they touch everything. It is not indifferent, even from the point of view of the special interests, to have official or independent representatives, as in the department as in the commune, and the alternative is forced, it makes take these from here or those from there. The *competent* candidate, outsider, beside and above the parties, is a lure, and the candidate without qualification has no reason to exist.

The departmental and communal interests do not have the same appearance, seen with glasses of different colors, and it is puerile to let it be believed that there are other than glasses of color.

The political question is therefore always, and with just reason, the dominant question for a virile nation; its disappearance is a sure sign of decadence.

That is my answer to the first objection. Let us approach the second.

It consists in asking whether the proposed divisions are not too numerous, if all are sufficiently justified, if the great parties, which the new scrutiny strikes, instead of being scrupulously represented, are not weakened and distorted; finally, and above all, whether the public education holds these distinctions.

Without hesitation, I reject the objection in its entirety and under each of its faces. Or these distinctions indeed exist in the country, and the Legislative Body - this mirror - must reflect them; or these party fractions have no consistency, and the scrutiny will do justice. Why remove them from authority? As for the weakness of the great parties, I do not distinguish the cause; is the ignorance of the elements of which they are composed the condition of their strength? It is an apparent force then, and an impotence. By my system, the great parties present themselves divided; but, if the points of divergence are known, the rallying points are known as well, and, in the hour of combat, the concentration is easy, and the combined action of the various bodies is prompt and decisive.

It remains the education for the universal suffrage: if it is to be done, which I grant without difficulty, it will be made better and faster under the pressure of necessity and by the exercise of a right whose power the elector will understand.

The universal suffrage, moreover, is not for me the Holy Ark, and at all I do not any opposition to one touch it.

This objection, which attaches itself to the classification, to the divisions and subdivisions of parties, if it was founded - and I do not think so, - my system keeps it intact. Whether it is preferable at present to count five parties instead of seven, or three instead of five, it certainly has its interest, but a transitory, momentary interest; there is convenience to proceed in a less radical manner, to do not first give a complete, rational organization to prepare the ground, we can support it: it is a detail of execution.

By the whole application of the system, the country will be represented absolutely, minorities and majority, man for man, as Stuart-Mill says; - by proceeding by temperament, though essential details can be lost, the great parties will have, in the Legislative Body, a value, an importance, and an authority far superior to those they have under the current system.

XIV

The universal suffrage needs to be directed. Although, this proposition, passed to the state of axiom, contains, however, two irreconcilable ideas; the need for direction can only be a transitory means or a criticism of the electoral law.

Let us observe, nearer, the directed universal suffrage.

They look for the elector, take him by the hand, lead him, give him a ballot that he would not have been able to choose, and, when this vote is taken, they bow before the verdict of the sovereign people.

It is the committee that arranges everything, concerts everything and prepares everything: the conviction, the understanding, the choice, the success. It has the ballots printed, it distributes them, it fills the electoral box... then it counts them with respect, one to one, and it calls them its will, the will of the country!

No! This man whose arms are moved is not an elector; he is only one who, without any suggestion, *wants* something and *knows* what he wants, emits an opinion, expresses a will, but he only appoints a representative.

That is the principle; it is placed, I know, on inaccessible heights: one cannot reach it. Let us try to get closer. With what clue can one to recognize the qualified voter? How does one sort them? Who will be contacted? Will it be the Director of Contributions? What is the amount where does the electoral capacity start? - In a primary teacher? What is the minimum compulsory education? - In a jury? How will it be composed? There are many question marks, many arbitrary answers: the data are lacking. This is not a problem to ask, it is a bias to take; in contrast to the system that demanded the *addition* of capacities, let us call for the *elimination* of incapacities.

I hear the protests: the equality! the right! the *natural* right!

The law is very contestable, and it is also very contested. If there existed, imperious, complete, whole, it would inscribe the miner and the idiot on the electoral lists; since it does not go so far, since it stops on the way, one can discuss it on the station.

How, in my vision, should the lists be composed? It is not in a few words that one can say it, and a long excursion into these bushes will take me too far from my subject; however, having asked the question with the obvious intention of leaving one to see my thought, I reply that the *first* radiation should be made... by the incapable themselves.

The voters would be offered a square of white paper and a pen: - he who can, this one will vote.

This electoral ballast, thrown into the sea, will singularly favor the march of the democratic vessel.

Wherever the average of instruction increases, the necessity of direction diminishes accordingly; One increasing incessantly, the other diminishing in the same measure; it is necessary to arrive at this level where, the balance being reached, the direction will be suppressed.

Therefore, the proposition that I am discussing might be formulated more accurately by means of a slight modification, with the intercalation of three words:

The universal suffrage needs, *as it stands*, to be directed.

I proceeded to the amputation of a part of the electorate, somewhat coldly, and, doubtless, in the opinion of some, a little brutally: what does it matter? This coldness, this firmness of surgeon, in no way exclude the sympathy for the patient, who will quickly recover his lost strength by the treatment I am pointing out.

If the elector, when will be going to the scrutiny, will have to go through the school door, it will have to be opened wide; he should not decree free and *compulsory* education, for words play in events a greater role than is believed, but simply he should recognize the right of children to education.

Germany and America have long preceded us in this path; the American Horace Mann, the founder of the common schools, said: "Every human creature has an *absolute right* to education; to refuse it is to condemn it to brutality and misery... Under a government like ours, it is indispensable that education should enable every citizen to fulfill his civil and social duties". And this is not the cause of innocent declamations, Moral obligation: the laws which intervened in Germany, they also intervened in the free America; the Massachusetts legislators punished with a fine of five pounds sterling, later raised to 40, parents and masters who were barbaric enough to deny their children or their apprentices an education that was considered the natural right of any intelligent creature"; and these laws, which are supposed to be oppressive, today without object, have fallen into disuse - failure of delinquents!

It is not new, indeed, even for our codes, it being only the right of the children: it is a matter of completing it.

The paternal power is fallen! The right of life and death of the Romans has left memories only in our classical tragedies, and the sale of children by the Gauls is almost relegated to the rank of fables.

Never, nevertheless, the French laws have sanctioned these excesses. The *Ordinances* and the *Customs* have always limited paternal authority; the *Constituent Assembly* considerably diminished it, and the

Code Napoleon reduced it to a mere tutelage of minor children.

Now, children, minors, are, by law, immune to ill-treatment; they are lodged, nourished, clothed... It is yet one step, it is the work of civilization that is developing.

The authority of the king and that of the father followed two parallel routes, marching at the same pace, diminishing at the same stages: whenever the discretionary power of the chief of State was shaken, the head of the family suffered a shock; or, changing the terms of the comparison, whenever the law has recognized a new right to the subject, to the father, it has, expressly or tacitly, registered an equivalent right for the child.

The right to vote granted to all the citizens of the age of twenty-one, *knowing how to read and write*, has as a corollary the right of children to *education*.

I do not depart, though it may seem, from the itinerary I have traced; this rapid glance at public instruction is not a distraction of travel, for my system is, at bottom, a *scale of votes* of an extreme sensibility, and the fluctuations of opinion will be so much the better expressed so much the ballots placed on the plates will have the same weight or the same value.

Let us now return to the question on the present terrain, and before the universal suffrage without any condition of capacity.

The voters may be divided into three series:

The first contains all those who live to any degree of the intellectual life, all those who are interested in the public affairs;

The second, particularly widespread in the countryside, completely strange to all the general facts, scarcely looks beyond the parish, and comprehends only the parochial questions;

The third - a quarter of the population! - in profound ignorance, does not know how to read or write!

Established these divisions, I am obliged to admit, the direction of the committees is necessary; and yet it is necessary to distinguish, there is always fagot and fagot, cases and cases.

That the committee directs, even by the hand, those who can not direct themselves with the eyes, I agree - this case of blindness explains, justifies its intervention; - but that it behaves in the same way with those who have a clear view and know where they are going, it is an abuse... to which the new system puts an end, for it deprives the committee of its only argument: success compromised if the votes are lost on a candidate other than its own.

Nothing is opposed, with the corrective of the *two simultaneous votes*, to the free organization of the committees, whose action will naturally change according to the environment in which they will act.

For the first series, the committee is simply an office that centralizes the information, discusses the candidates, indicates its preferences and takes the necessary steps to ensure the sincerity of the vote or to note the illegalities: - it is an agency.

For the other two series, the committee is a center of active, ardent and passionate propaganda; for, in order to raise the illiterate and apathetic masses, there must be a lever that is otherwise energetic: it is a direction.

It does not follow from these divisions that each series *belongs* to an opinion or a committee. I try to define the role of the committees and not to classify the parties; they have, or ought to have, their separate committees, which address to all voters, and such committees are, here or there, at the same time, simple office of information for some, centers of propaganda for the others.

These are the committees as I understand them, taking into account the current state of affairs and ignoring our electoral law or the decree that supplements it.

The French law, suspicious and *protectionist*, watches the electors and the committees; it holds them to the distance, closely related: in reality, it does not protect either these or those; it hampers them equally. It is wrong, because it intervenes where it does not have to do it, because the relations between the voters and the committees look exclusively at the committees and the voters.

Committees, freed from the tangled web of bureaucratic regulations and articles scattered throughout our codes, should be able to meet as often and in such numbers as they deem necessary.

They should above all be able to organize themselves freely from a financial point of view, for the elections will have a character truly democratic only when they are made by voluntary subscriptions at the expense of the electors.

These costs are considerable and can prevent many honorable candidates from performing. It is not a popular law, one in which one can read by thought this article not voted, but it is in the place: In the interior of the empire, without conditions of domicile and cense, all the rentiers, capitalists, great proprietors, etc., are eligible. No, fortune is not a privilege, especially in France, where equality is so well understood - by the inferiors!

Another consideration, all moral adds a decisive weight to one that precedes it: the money spread here and there, hands full, without counting, by a candidate, whatever his personal worth and the purity of his intentions, greatly resembles electoral corruption - to the point that it is sometimes misunderstood -, while, on the part of the electors or the committee, it is only a patriotic gift, a sacrifice necessary for the success of the cause.

XV

I have already, incidentally, on the subject of the committees, affirmed that the enfranchisement of the electors is one of the consequences of the application of my system. The flag of independence, planted on the classical ground of discipline, is a very new fact, enough to make it worthwhile to stop there.

I will try to put this fact in full light, to show these freedmen at work.

Private meetings are held in a circumscription. The access is not interdicted, so let us enter. - The first, composed solely of conservatives, is legitimately presided by Dr. Pangloss; the assembly, convinced that everything is for the best under the best of the governments, approves without restraint, admires without reserve, and always finds *sufficient reason* for the laws and decrees that protect the sleep of the Empire. Unanimity in satisfaction! - In the second, the champions of the *right-wing*, contemplating with sadness the ruins piled up by our revolutions, are clustered around two columns, the capitals no longer existing; one still reads on the chipped bases: hereditary kingship, State religion. Unanimity in the complaint! - In the third, the disrespectful ones of the *left wing* claim tumultuously the primordial rights, the liberties anterior and superior to the constitutions. Unanimity in the revindication!

If at each meeting the voters had to resolve only the fundamental question, all would agree taking the hat off: one would not meet a dissident; unfortunately, what comes is the accessory question, which divides them. Who will be the advocates to defend, to make prevail, the principles on which they all agree?

This accessory question, as one knows, brings the main question to the present method of voting; it is the only one that seems to be posed to the voters.

Let us go on. The electoral circumscription is entitled to six deputies; there are twenty candidates. Then the ardent, passionate, injurious, envenomed discussions arise; then the coteries have a fine game; then the intractable and the violent overwhelm the timid; and, as the success itself of the cause depends on the success of the candidate, the most intelligent, the most devoted ones, make the sacrifice of their preferences, and, yielding to necessity, magnify the cortege of the leaders.

Pushed, pressed, surrounded, impotent, the elector votes as the majority wants, or as a coterie wants, or as the intractable ones want; rarely as, intimately, personally, he really wants. He votes reluctantly, sometimes for an ambitious third order, sometimes even for an intriguer, whom he knows to be an intriguer!

Tired of this servitude, desirous of getting rid of all those clan chiefs who dispose of his will, I suppose an elector conveying and uniting these three political groups to friendly submit to them some observations:

We form here, he would say, three divided parties: one of these parties asks, without taking the trouble to enumerate them, all the liberties; the other, more discreet, requires only a few; the other is satisfied with those it has. I will not tell you what my place is among you; this statement would be useless, since the proposition I have to do is in the common interest. You, Conservatives, if you are in the majority in the circumscription, you will want to be in the majority in the deputation, nothing more just; you, voters of the right and left, majority or minority, you want your share also. Well! Let us count ourselves! Let us first settle this first point, and, with this essential question emptied, we will take care of the candidates. Each of us, then, without preoccupation with the result, without any unpleasant compromise, even without prior agreement with the neighbors, will vote, in his independence, for the man he deems most worthy of representing him.

Let us intercalate here the *Very good! - That's it! - You are right! -* of the parliamentary reports. The orator, encouraged, continues thus:

Choosing our candidates, we are only aware of our conscience; we should not account the vote for the person! In this way, not only will we all be proportionally represented as political groups, but also our deputies will be appointed by us, voters, and not by our committees!

Let us prove it!

The Conservatives will write the names of their candidates on white ballot papers; the partisans of the right on green bulletins, and those of the left, naturally, on red bulletins. Once the ballot is over, the triage will be done: so many white ballots, so many green, and so many reds. This is the answer to the main question, that on which there is conformity of opinion, unanimity. How many white deputies, how many greens, how many reds? This is an easy account to do. As for our lawyers, as for the candidates - incidental question - those who, in each group, without pressure, spontaneously, have obtained the greatest number of votes, will represent us in the Legislative Body.

What this elector would say is what I have already said myself; the system he would propose is the one I have outlined; these multicolored bulletins are those of which I have given the model.

Indeed:

I vote first for my party; it is necessary to affirm it, to establish its numerical strength, to demonstrate its power, to claim the part of influence due to it; and my ballot, *whatever names I add, is counted for my party*. I then vote freely for my candidates, for those I have chosen, personally chosen. *There are no lost votes*, no reason of discipline hangs over my determination.

What matters the committees, the newspapers, and the meetings? They do not direct now, they counsel, and these counsels, I listen to them, no doubt, but I discuss them, and I am not bound to follow them.

My freedom is such that I can put on my bulletin bearing the motto *left* one or more candidates from the *government* or from the *right* - personal sympathy, esteem, consideration for great character or for great talent - without this vote of esteem, affection, respect to damage in any way the success of my cause, without there being a single lost vote in total.

My whole bulletin bears its color; it is given to my party. I detach a name that profits only an individual: my affections have not been wounded, and my party is not diminished.

If the independence of the elector and the right of minorities are assured, out of contestation, another consequence of the application of my system is that these same minorities are represented throughout the duration of the powers of the Legislative Body, regardless of the vacancies that may occur.

The list system, as it has been practiced so far, does not include partial re-elections; the system of electoral colleges of *three corners*, adopted in England, include them much less, since the outgoing member, if he belongs to the minority, that is to say, if he owed his appointment to a protective suit, is fatally replaced by a member of the majority. This contradiction did not, however, arrest the English Parliament, and, in the privileged circumscription, where the deputy had prevailed, under the new law, one-third plus one, it is allowed to nominate a member of an opposite opinion, to the shelter of the old law kept, of half plus one!

The system that I propose prevents these inconveniences; by voting simultaneously for a party and for candidates, one draws up at the same time the list of deputies and substitutes.

The resignation of a deputy, his death, etc., logically bring to the Legislative Body the candidate who, in the same circumscription and on the same list, has arrived, in the order of the votes obtained, immediately after the last deputy appointed.

The same applies to the multiple elections.

It does not follow from this that the duration of the powers of the deputies must extend or be not reduced. Of course not. The universal suffrage calls for a considerable number of new voters every year, and each year death makes large erasures on the electoral lists. This renewal, so rapid, so profound, without even taking into account the events and variations of opinion, imperiously demands, on the contrary, the frequency of general elections.

XVI

Free in his preferences, in front of the committees, as when facing his party, the elector will enjoy, nevertheless, only a theoretical independence, if he is not protected from administrative pressure. This pressure, almost without effect in the great centers, increases as one moves away from them, and put all its power in the confines of the department. Thus the liberal opposition, triumphant in the main city, is generally beaten in the country.

The influences are a little more balanced in the cities: if the mayor speaks, the committees answer; if the mayor leans on one side, the municipal council leans on the other; each party has its agents, its newspaper, its murals: everything is done in public, under the constant control of an energetic population, jealous of its rights.

In the small towns, the administration reigns without sharing; the opposition rarely finds there an agent to distribute its bulletins, a wall to paste its posters!

Since, in the electoral battles, the victory belongs to the big battalions, it is prudent to watch the enrollment, in order to know exactly the way in which the companions of countrymen, so numerous, giving with so much union, crushing all the resistances, are raised.

In France, on 37,548 communes, there are about 28,000 that do not count, on average, more than 120 electors; - the protests addressed to the Legislative Body has given an overview of the situation placed to them.

I am talking about the moral situation, and I leave in the shadows the ballot boxes, without questioning the security of the voters, when the votes are placed in the mayor's bedroom, without astonishing me by their fertility when there are more ballots than voters.

The mayor, assisted at some distance by the judge of the peace, the parish priest, the rural guard, the gendarme, awaits confidentially his municipal agents, furnished with ballots attached to their cards by means of a pin.

One can imagine the embarrassment of the elector, especially if, in addition to the official ballot, he carries another - the ballot deemed seditious - that he would like to slip into the ballot box. How can he be saved from mistrustful looks? Folded in four, rolled between his fingers, this ballot, he believes at least, is of such transparency that everyone reads through it: the mayor, the judge of the peace, the rural guard and the gendarme!

He sees, presiding over the electoral office, the mayor stretching out his hand to examine the paper that is given him, in order to assure... that there is only one vote cast, and, confused, trembling, disturbed, substituting for the seditious ballot the pinned ballot, he approaches like a culprit - and votes like an innocent!

I resolutely dismiss, like the Legislative Body, without wishing to verify them, all the facts mentioned in the documents whose signatures are not legalized: prefectural posters, false news, sensational news, threats, etc. I retain only the difficulty of putting into the hands of the mayor a vote contrary to the opinion of the mayor.

Shall one say that the vote is secret? No, that is a good argument for the tribune! There is no need to unfold a ballot to read it. The result of the election, in each office, is known before the counting of the ballots.

Those who, Mr. de Montalembert ahead, supported the vote in the commune were, however, somewhat misled: They intended to deliver of the count half to the castellans of the country and to the priest; - the administration has kept most of it! The rural commune, feeble, credulous, impressionable, curves, obedient, under these three influences, sometimes counteracting itself, but more ordinarily pushing it in the same direction. It is exalted by chimerical promises; it is frightened by placing before its eyes an old decoration, refreshed from time to time, and representing the red horizon of revolutions!

How to subtract the voters from the vigilance of these interested tutors? By calling them to the chief township of the canton (except to the main city of the department), in the midst of an electoral storm; There, agitated, shaken by the four winds, swept away by the reaction, brought back by freedom, they will fortify themselves in the struggle, they will learn to deposit without constraint, in a well kept urn, a ballot actually chosen by them!

The vote in the main city of the canton is the essential article to be inserted in a new electoral law.

XVII

We have just gone, in all directions, through the narrow circle around the problem of the representation of the minorities. This circle, this limited and circumscribed land, let us compare it to a dwelling we would like to acquire; it will be, in fact, a very convenient dwelling for the universal suffrage, and it would be acquired at the expense of the absolute power. - After having successively examined the various stages - the right of minorities, freedom of vote, new organization of the committees, vote in the main city of the canton, electoral competence - after having, we say, visited the interior, let us open the windows, and look a little outside.

Here, first, in the distance, scarcely perceived, the question of *parliamentary* coalitions is present. Let us not forget - this is an essential starting point - that *electoral* coalitions are virtually abolished by my system. But, it is said, the coalition is only displaced: removed from the electoral body, it enters the Chamber with the deputies; the rigid law of the majority, the majority plus one, necessarily reigns in a deliberative assembly; the minorities are impotent, it is natural that they should be supported: one will see there the parliamentary coalitions being restored.

Let us see first what they were; after we shall see what they may be.

So much we recall today the stormy questions that raised so many discussions and swept the ministries: hereditary appanages, dowry of the Princess Louise, evacuation of Ancona, secret funds, etc.

Alas! There are only proper names, names known to all, which ring in memory.

When one looks at thirty years of his own self, at that favorable distance in which the details that deceive contemporaries are lost in the shadow, in which only the characteristic salient facts can be distinguished, the only thing striking is the furious assault given to a dismantled citadel - the power! What a spectacle! A confused melee of ministers and deputies on the steps leading to the Tuileries; fierce struggle between some thirty grave figures: some are overthrown, wounded by contradictions, bruised by the balls of the ballot, torn by speeches; the others are exhausted, but also bruised and powdery.

It is a mock-heroic poem, a variant of *Le Lutrin*; the infolio of Barbin is replaced by ministries.

The scandal has been immense - and fatal to the parliamentary government.

Let us specify the origin and the cause; let us quote for this inquiry a witness and, according to the fashionable neologism, an authorized witness (1):

"The elections were held in 1837, not as a public struggle between the great opinions and the great parties of the country, but as a confused mix of candidates supported or rejected by the administration, as they were presumed favorable or contrary.

"From these elections, thus made without certain principles and without a flag deployed, a disorganized Chamber emerged, strange to *firm and public engagements*, dominated by individual interests and feelings..."

And further:

"Under such auspices, the elections (1839) were ardently challenged and accomplished in a great pell-mell of opinions and alliances (...); they gave the coalition a limited, however, obvious victory, etc."

The conditions are no longer the same! The deputy from the rational vote and the free vote is the agent of a party: there is a program which he cannot deviate from, he is took by *firm and public engagements*, he arrives at the Legislative Body with an *imperative mandate*, broad, but precise. - The ballot paper is nothing else: - it was not Mr. Cochin, Mr. Thiers, or Mr. Picard who was appointed; it is above all a member of the *right*, the *third party* or the *left*.

The vote of the deputies is foreseen, obliged, and the vote is public; for if the secret scrutiny is understood when it is the guarantee of the independence of the voter, - and this is the case of the elector, - it is inadmissible when the voter must account to the country of his actions, - and this is the case of the deputy. Under certain circumstances, no doubt, momentary co-operation is possible between the various parts of the House: thus the liberals of all shades may unite with the Catholics to obtain the *necessary liberties*; as in the Roman question, the Catholics with the third party for the preservation of the temporal power of the Pope. - But in what is this agreement in the vote, resulting from agreement in thought, contrary to the most scrupulous loyalty?

This co-operation in defense of a common idea has nothing to do with the parliamentary league of 1838, and this is impossible.

The prior deputy, himself a product of a coalition of voters, and privileged voters, a personal candidate, independent (the roles are interchanged: here the deputies are independent, there, the voters), was free to become the instrument of an ambition; the new deputy, appointed by a party and by the universal suffrage, does not belong to himself. A political or religious question being asked - irrespective of the minister who supports it, and even if a hostile poll should lead to its retirement, - he shall vote in accordance with the prescriptions of the ballot paper, in accordance with this imperative, he votes on the question and not on the minister.

Obviously, the rejection of a ministerial proposal always defeats the ministry, but the terms are no longer the same: it is a principle that triumphs over another principle, the majority of the House that gives another direction to the politics, it is the country that, not approving what the minister has done or proposes to do, appoints another official more skillful, or understands him better; this is, in short, the most precious resource of the parliamentary government - it *detains* the situation.

(1) Guizot. *Memories for serve to the history of my time.*

XVIII

The parties have not, hitherto, a very fixed significance; inflated beyond the measure, increased of threats or illusions for some, empty for others, they have, for all, the wrong to evade to serious examination. According to the skeptics, the opposition has the sad and vain task of contradicting everything, as the officials are in the hard obligation of approving everything. According to the believers, the opposition is in a position to realize immediately - and by decrees - the dreams hatched in the kingdom of Utopia: it is the golden age, it is the universal peace with its cornucopia of abundance; it is the embrace of the enemy brothers, *yours and mine*; it is the extinction of pauperism... Certainly these imputations are false; these hopes are chimerical; only, who has the fault if they are so widespread? Those who misunderstand or those who half understand?

What is the Catholic Party? What does it want? What are the third party, the left, and the radicals? What do they want? No doubt, their tendencies are not unknown; their evolutions are explained; but from that twilight to the great and beautiful sun that I like and that it will take place, there is a distance. It is not enough to rely on some general principles, which everyone accepts and everyone - alas! - interprets; it is not enough to say: We are the party of law, or the parliamentary party, or the party of the national sovereignty; for I have some difficulty in seeing the three parties, for I can weld these expressions one to the other under which they assert themselves, mingle them, and enclose them in a single formula: national sovereignty is the law expressed by the parliamentary government.

These cutting affirmations, taken in isolation, do not cut anything at all. - The right! It is, for the party that invokes it more especially, the succession to the throne reserved for the legitimate heir; it is also, for another party, the faculty that the people have to place on this same throne he who the people wish. - The right! It is the temporal sovereignty, it is the spiritual independence of the Pope; it is also the sovereignty and the independence of the Romans - The parliamentary government! It is the direction of the affairs confined to the assembly of the representatives of the nation, an assembly resulting from the universal suffrage or from limited suffrage, having above it an emperor, a king, or a president; beside it the Senate or the Chamber of peers, or having nothing above or next to it. National sovereignty! It goes from the parliamentary government, with which it merges, to the permanent and armed clubs!

The great principles contain all that one wishes to put into it, and what one wishes to put into it will be well to detail.

If the parties gave a list of the reforms, of the laws themselves that seem to them useful, necessary; if they summarized them in a program large enough to contain the individual disagreements, precise enough so that no one was mistaken about the purpose for follow-up, the parties, enlightened by a new day, would cause less fright and be judged with more equity.

The candidate, instead of presenting himself to the electors as the champion of public liberties, of public morality, as the defender of the family, of religion, of property; instead of aligning words that are hollow, would simply submit a program, at the head of which would the urgent question be, the question of the moment, that which gives a special character to each election.

The free countries, I mean those who know how to deal with their affairs, while maintaining all their political divisions, do not proceed any other way. To quote only recent examples, the Americans -*Democrats* and *Republicans* - have long enough aimed, until the solution, the question of slavery; and the English - *Tories* and *Whigs* - sometimes the electoral reform, and sometimes the abolition of the Church of Ireland, also went to the solution.

In France - for a large party at least - is not the electoral freedom the main issue, the question of the moment? Are not the reforms that the same party demanded, for the most part, not sufficiently studied, intended (let us reserve those which are discussed)? Finally, the adoption or rejection of such a program by the majority of voters would not this deliver us from the uncertainties of the situation?

The road to progress is full of detours and surprises; it sometimes brings us back to the point of departure. I thought I was approaching the free cities of the future, and here I have just mentioned Athens and Rome before the Christian era!

It is because the direct vote of the law is the democratic form par excellence; it is the natural form.

Here is Athens! Let us say: "Citizens are trained for the duty of both speaker and listener, and each man, while feeling that he exercises his share of influence on the decision, identifies his own safety and his own happiness with the vote of the majority and become familiar with the notion of a sovereign authority, to which it cannot and must not resist". (1)

The law proposed is discussed clause by clause; every citizen intervening in the debate, be by a speech, be by a word, be by a gesture, be otherwise. - Applauses, cries, boos; - all the spectators are actors. Holding the session, one approves, one criticizes, one deliberates, one concludes.

But what was easy in Athens, in small republics, is not so in a great country like France: the inevitable frequency of these assemblies will require continual displacements, and the Place de la Concorde, in lieu of the Agora, difficultly will contain and collect the ten million voters spread over a vast territory.

Here is Rome! The *plebiscite* - a decision taken by the plebs, at least at the beginning - plays an immense role: the Forum is full of ardent citizens; the orators succeed without interruption - not without being interrupted - in the tribune of harangues. This staging, embellished by the imagination, these fiery tribunes, this sovereignty of the citizen, visible, effective, have an invincible attraction for French democracy.

I do not intend - far from it! - to present the Greek or Roman institutions as good models to imitate: improvised decisions leave too great part to the unforeseen, to the subterfuges, to the lies, to the ravishment; the history of the popular assemblies is too often a series of retractions. The prodigies of the skill do not prove the clairvoyance of those who allow themselves to be taken, and the prodigies of eloquence do not always bring the triumph of justice. - I am for the reflected vote and not for the enthusiastic vote.

The plebiscite, today, it is true, has a more tranquil appearance. The silent pen replaced the tongue; the advertising replaced the noise. The question asked is delivered to the meditation of the country... But this question, who poses it? Who writes it? - He who has an interest in solving it by the affirmative.

The alternative is only apparent; the population, consulted, has only the faculty of accepting what is proposed to it.

What will be the proposition? - The choice of a king? The form of a government? These things are designated in advance - the *yes* is easy; the *no* is not a solution: it is the unknown, the anarchy, the civil war. The same is true for a constitution, a monument all in one piece, to be taken or abandoned: the *yes* is always easy for the one who finds it by fact; but this *yes* is too absolute for a certain number of citizens, and the *no* does not allow others to indicate what they would have liked. - *Yes*, less this or that article. *No*, I prefer this or that.

The proposal prejudges the issue.

And, nevertheless, the plebiscitary regime is rational: voting for things is infinitely better than voting for people.

It is the reconciliation between the two principles: voting for things and voting for people, the plebiscitary regime and the delegation, which my system hopes to achieve. Its application would develop this double character; the parties will disengage more and more from the mist that envelops them, and the deputies will gain consideration; one will vote freely for someone, clearly for something.

Though the designations *third party*, *left*, *radicals*, etc., understood and accepted, allow voters to classify and manifest, if not their opinions on pending issues, at least their tendencies; although the present constitution of the parties is sufficient for the functioning of my system; although these parties, entering Parliament in proportional numbers, as they are in the country, the Parliament faithfully and completely represent the majority and the minorities - I think it is good to insist on the advantages of the political program, which I propose only as an improvement, as a desirable complement, as a means of giving the public opinion a sound and a practical direction.

Will the difficulty of drafting a program be alleged? The disarray of principles? The inconsistency of the parties? The public ignorance? The incompetence of the universal suffrage?

This indictment, partly true, partly false, is the same as has been drawn up for all the peoples at all the times. We are worth no less, perhaps we are worth a little more; *perhaps* it is the only concession I grant. - What! We would be incapable of choosing, of preferring one law to another! Before a proposition, between the *yes* and the *no*, we would remain puzzled - like the donkey of Buridan! We will not know to do in the nineteenth century what the Athenians did in the time of Pericles, what the Romans did in the days of the Gracchi!

Let us employ the infallible process to dispel the ghosts: let us approach the scarecrow until we touch it with the hand, until we laugh at our fright. - Does the voter, for example, have no opinion on the question of official nominations? Does not the right of assembly have its supporters and opponents? Is the responsibility of civil servants, free education, the appointment of mayors by municipal councils so vague that they exceed the average level of the universal suffrage?

I pass over without detaining more on the objection, and, in order to render my proposition more striking, I shall write two programs of authority; they will not be complete, and I cannot guarantee their complete accuracy. These two points are without object for the use I want to make of them.

POLITICAL PROGRAMS

CENTER LEFT	LEFT
PARLIAMENTARY GOVERNMENT	REPRESENTATION OF THE COUNTRY BY THE COUNTRY
CENTRALIZATION	DECENTRALIZATION

------------------ ------------------

MAIN QUESTION	**MAIN QUESTION**
Supression of the official candidacies	ELECTORAL FREEDOM
	Suppression of the official candidacies.
	Free organization of the committees.
	Right of assembly without restriction.
	Vote in the capital of the department.
	Delimitation of circumscriptions by the Legislative Body.

------------------ ------------------

REFORMS TO BE OBTAINED	REFORMS TO BE OBTAINED
Nomination of mayors by the public power but elected by the municipal councils.	Nomination of mayors by the municipal councils.
Delimitation of circumscriptions by the general councils.	Press offenses referred to the jury.
	Free public education.
	Children's right to instruction.
	Responsibility of functionaries.
(?)	Freedom of teaching.
	Religious liberty.
(?)	Separation Church-State.
	Social reforms left to the
(?)	initiative of the citizens by the complete freedom of
(?)	associations.
	Etc., etc.

Let us suppose that these programs are exact - the *whites* also have their meaning. If my ballot bears the designation *center left*, I am almost satisfied with the imperial regime, and I draw the attention of the government to the abolition of the official nominations, the delimitation of the circumscriptions. If my ballot bears the designation *left*, I am obviously asking, first of all, for the broadest electoral freedom and, in addition, for a profound reorganization of our institutions: the responsibility of the functionaries and the separation of the Church and the State, etc.

Thus, to vote for his party is to vote for a political program, for certain reforms, for a set of laws; - the electoral verdict is the new form of the plebiscite: it is the plebiscite of the majority of the electors, annotated, amended, and contained by the minorities; it is the national sovereignty in its most rational manifestation. With this extension, the new vote - double vote, one applying to a political program, the other to a candidate - will become the *plebiscite vote*.

(1) G. Grote

XIX

The precise knowledge of the state of the public opinion is, for the government that is inspired by it, the first, if not the only, condition of its duration. It is a question here only of free people, or who have been, or wish to be so.

It is a truth easy to prove to the readers, but will long remain at the door of the royal palaces.

Sovereigns, statesmen, ministers are intimately and firmly persuaded that a nation must live and think in a certain way - the way that suits them. They themselves are the wise men among the wise: from the rectitude of their judgment to the infallibility, there is not distance.

All initiative is due to them; they grant liberties, to a certain extent, and, to a just extent, they know our irresponsible, disorderly appetite, and they put us to the regime - imperial regime. They know what milk to feed us. - They have their test tube! - Then they naturally think of fortify their power; they take some guarantees: first this one, then this other, then this other again; they are part of the nation, and they do their part.

With the things thus arranged, they do not doubt the general satisfaction; therefore every complaint a little noisy, every criticism a little alive, takes the proportion of an attempt, and the attempt is vigorously pursued; because they are justice based on force, because legal representation is with them, the administration is with them, the army is with them!

Nevertheless, there is one day when the representation no longer knows what it represents, where the administration is disturbed, where the army hesitates, and then... then the triumphant revolution, knowing neither what it wants nor what it can, violently introduces into the country a new regime, which has only an ephemeral duration.

If the sovereigns could, from the heights where they stand, perceive the profound changes in society; if they knew how the words they deign to pronounce are received, how their reasons are weighed and how much frivolous they are found, how the people, ironic and mistrustful, treat them from equal to equal, perhaps they would decide to get closer to the crowd, to mingle, adopting the ideas and costumes of their time.

The chief of the State, instead of being the *chief*, the *head*, that is to say, the one who commands, that is to say, the one who thinks for everyone, would become, by a more reduced meaning of the word, the first, the principal, which would not be a mediocre honor. No longer representing the divine majesty, but the majority of the country, moving like him, following him forward and back, he would conform its more tranquil existence to the exigencies of a new situation.

It has been said, I know, and without recoiling before the expression, that a prince like this, deprived of all initiative and power, will be nothing else than... *a pig at the fattening*! I do not agree; but, returning to the proposition, I ask that, deprived also of all power and initiative, he might be one of the people!

If the same fact causes the same comparison, if this bestial role is, inevitably, the lot of one or the other, it is dangerous, it seems to me, to present the alternative and to ask for our preference!

Fortunately, that's not a joke; the prince who genuinely consults the country, who conscientiously studies how to translate into action its desire legally expressed, in default of the title of great man, will deserve that of a great citizen - which is better.

Do I need to remark that the qualification of a *prince*, employed without intention, contains, in my opinion, no privilege, no grace of state? - Far from there! - I am full of deference to the President of the United States, Abraham Lincoln, the son of a pioneer; I am full of mistrust before a great personage whose birth has been saluted by twenty-one cannon-shots. - An indiscreet question wanders over my lips: if he were not a prince, what would he be?

More comfortable after this explanation, I repeat: with the head of state - a woodcutter or a prince - faithfully executing the measures voted by a national assembly, a mathematical reduction of the electorate, the public tranquility is assured; the revolts will lack a pretext, the revolutions will have no object.

A revolution! -- Why? For the majority? But it governs. - From a minority? But how could it be fulfilled?

In profit of the *chief*, there is a little less than a *coup d'etat*; it is a matter of the Assembly to make it impossible; it is a matter of the country not to undergo it. And, even, why this hypothesis? When there is doubt as to the state of mind, when each party, irritated, thinks it represents the immense majority of the nation; when one cannot verify, on this propitious night one conceives the coup d'etat, the savior! - But in broad daylight, and against the express will of the same nation, who will dare to tempt it?

In 1848, by the very declaration of the republicans, the republic was violence against France, and even Paris, which proclaimed it, accepted it rather than wanted it.

One knows the consequences of that surprise: during six months a republic anxious, frightened, the trouble in the minds, the riot in the street; for three years, a nominal republic, the monarchists everywhere, dominating everywhere, and publicly disputing the succession of the regime that was crumbling.

This reaction was legitimate; but let us understand it. France was wrong - it is my opinion - in repulsing the republican institutions. It had tried a monarchy adapted to various dynasties; it had tried the dictatorship, of the legitimacy and of the quasi-legitimacy: what risk would it make by trying logic? But, panic-stricken, irritated, especially by having been consulted on a *fait accompli*, denying its adhesion, in its blind anger it experienced a singular pleasure in breaking and demolishing what had been built without it or in spite of it. Now, although it was wrong, as France was, it was its right to be wrong.

Instead of deputies appointed by the voters, suppose, in the month of February, 1848, a Chamber elected by universal suffrage, my system functioning (I admit, although unlikely then, the events that brought about revolution and revolution itself); suppose this House, a faithful representation of the country, giving manifest proof, by the enumeration of the parties, that the *extreme left* is, in reality, only an insignificant minority: would it have been possible - even among Parisians - to install the republic? The thought would not have come to them.

Let us make the contrary supposition: the composition of the Chamber - by the Chamber I always mean the country - establishing the indisputable preponderance of the republican left, and the revolution becoming legitimate and salutary; - the republic would have been legally proclaimed and sincerely and definitively accepted.

The conclusion is thus: no revolution: perfect agreement between the government and the country, that is, the government of the country by the country, stability and security;

Or, putting the things at the worst, an easy, legitimate revolution, with a definite purpose and the assent of the majority, that is to say, a revolution freely desired and bearing the fruits expected of it, in other words, again - stability and security.

XX

I have finished.

The exhibition of my system, preceded and followed by discussions and comments, is finished; I have nothing more to add... except that a good part of these discussions and comments was useless: I could dispense myself with repeating banal truths, and explain at length what had been understood from the first word.

This excuse given - good or bad - and accepted for what it is worth, having given the part of the fire (it is the case to say it!), it lacks only to conclude.

Is the program completed? Is the problem solved?

By removing the interrogative form, the answer, it seems to me, is contained in the question.

The problem is solved, and the solution *naturally* emerged from new guaranties that maintain to every political manifestation a double character of freedom and sincerity.

I remind them:

1. The impossibility of coalitions;
2. The abolition of the dictatorship of the committees;
3. The complete freedom of the elector.

This reform will profoundly modify our electoral habits and customs.

We will have nothing to do with this victorious argument used by all the parties, that the public opinion is with them: instead of those imaginary populations that the orator pretends to see and boldly displays to his opponents, he will have the reality, sometimes ironic, that is to say, the table of the census of the votes; instead of a mirage that he can embellish, an addition that he can verify.

We will understand finally what these noises say, confused up to the present, and which are called *votes*, for these votes will articulate words; - one counted them, one would listen to them.

The minorities will indeed be minorities; impotent, not discouraged, they will call by the future. But the present will be conquered by the majority, and the majority, satisfied by a legitimate preponderance, out of discussion, will make in a just measure to the minorities, relegated to the second and third plans, the concessions that the situation will admit, since the exposed system is an instrument whose precision cannot be disputed.

"If the Chamber were open to all, on equal terms, the minorities, always ambitious to produce themselves, would attach themselves to a regime in which the right would be guaranteed. But what can a democrat, a liberal, a worker do in this or that province? What does his vote - that beforehand he knows useless - matter to him? What does a Chamber from which his opinion is necessarily excluded make for him? Let us make every vote equal in value, that *every elector be sure that his vote will weigh in the scale*, that the same number of votes will make a deputy throughout France, and be sure that the elections will be more closely followed and less ardent, and that *the decisions of the ballot will be accepted with more confidence and respect by all opinions"*.

Although the quoted lines seem a natural consequence of the considerations already given, although they complement them, I humbly admit that they do not belong to me. I borrow them from Mr. Edouard Laboulaye, whose authority in these matters comes to my aid. What I was about to say, Mr. Edouard Laboulaye had already said, and very well said. I have profited; under an opinion that I consider to be a good one, I had to put an unknown name: - I had my signature legalized.

POST SCRIPTUM
August 21, 1869.

During the printing of this volume, events succeeded each other with such rapidity that, if my intention had been to prepare a work of polemic or combat, arguments and projectiles would produce no effect, the adversary having transformed his means of defense.

We have just witnessed a spectacle that was thought to be indefinitely adjourned - the crowning of the building. - This delicate work could not be carried out without damage to the Constitution. - It was for the Constitution, it seems, as the egg of Columbus: one could not hold it standing without breaking it a little. What does it matter? Here it is well seated, as one uses to say.

This work of consolidation, nevertheless, interests me thriftily: a Constitution, even perfectible, has only a relative importance; it is worth what the country that accepts it is worth, what its representatives, who interpret it, are worth; moreover, a good electoral system is, for me, more valuable than a good Constitution.

I, at least here, have not to appreciate the new reforms. How are they produced? How do they relate to the electoral manifestation? It is here the only question to be examined, and, in this order of ideas, the history of these last three months is curious and instructive.

On the day following the vote, on 26 May, the Minister of the Interior sent to the mayors lords the following telegraphic dispatch:

"The result of the elections is known in 280 of the 292 circumscriptions. The number of deputies appointed in the circumscriptions where the government has supported the candidates and in those where it has observed neutrality amounts to 196. There is tie in 58 circumscriptions.

"The deputies belonging to the opposition, re-elected or elected for the first time, are to the number of 26."

That is, therefore, the conservative majority - an overwhelming majority - reconstituted! We are finding there the veterans of the great army, the good and solid troops that followed the government to Mexico, which would not have been shrunk in a second expedition to *the interior*. - Opposite to this, one sees the minority, a handful, composed of the volunteers of the... freedom, ill-equipped, without uniforms, undisciplined; but full of ardor, of enthusiasm, of hopes, bold until the imprudence, brave until the temerity. In a camp the national flag floats, showing the eagles; in the other, the same flag, unrolled at the third only, and giving a new Lamartine the opportunity of uttering a new speech.

The third party has disappeared. - The reaction and the revolution are present!

The second round of the scrutiny, as expected, reinforces the opposition of some thirty members; the situation of the belligerents, as it seems, almost did not change.

The speech of the camp of Chalons, the letter to Baron de Mackau, the great collar to Baron J. David, indicate the preferences of the government. The hostilities will begin; France, attentive, moved, anxious, - waits!

The deputies are summoned for the verification of the powers... they arrive. - Suddenly, the scene changes. - The veil that concealed the secrecy of the elections falls, one does not know how... and one discovers - employing, by the effect of surprise, an old-fashioned expression - that *France is center left*!

This revelation imposes itself upon the world at once: the radicals retire, silent, on the summit of the mountain; the great army, immovable, unresolved, devastated by intestine divisions, watches, in terror, the sparkling star of the third party appearing in the political sky.

Pushed by the ever-rising tide of opinion, put in front of the government as to an opponent, the third party, very decided to ask for concessions - and the need to make it - writes, not without difficulty, an interpellation to that which come to rally the defectors of the majority.

The emperor himself, lost at first into the plains of the reaction, meets his road to Damascus: the divine voice exalts him, he sends his message... and prorogues the Chamber.

The scene changes again... In the interval of recollection that separates the decree of prorogation from the presentation of the *senatus consultum* in the Senate, the signification of the elections is more than ever disputed. The Catholic party, compiling the professions of faith of the deputies, declares that the majority was acquired by it. The left also verifies the electoral record: all things considered, the country is with it! Then it tries to condense its grievances into a unique and harmonious protest, and, failing, it publishes thirty of them all different. The third party, surprised in its own audacity and acknowledging that he was somewhat far, nevertheless recalls, with a legitimate pride, its effective interpellation, the 116 signatures given and the five or six rejected. As for the official party, recovered from its fright, laughing with a loud throat, and thereby showing the teeth, it proved its strength by the nomination of the members of the bureau.

At the last table - the last known - the curtain rises on the Senate.

The President (Mr. Rouher), in a temperate speech, announces: "The modifications that *seem* to have been prepared by a happy agreement between the Government and the Legislative Corps."

"*Seem*" would be a pearl if the speech was a jewel case!

More constitutional, the Minister of Justice and Religious Affairs (Mr. Duvergier) adds that, by presenting the draft of the *senatus consultum*, the Emperor *believes it is advisable to propose* these reforms.

One follows the reading of the project: the responsibility of the ministers, the right of interpellation, the right of amendments, the initiative of the laws, the veto of the Senate, etc., etc.

This is, thus, the definitive interpretation of the electoral manifestation! What do we know? Who guarantees it exactly? How did the government get there? Which unknown parts, what secret reports, what documents did he consult?

Did it give in under the threat of interpellation? Childish fear! - The group of the third party, skillfully launched, rolling on the slopes of the ministries, had grown rapidly like the snowball; but, like the snow, it was destined to melt rapidly: a little resistance, and it stopped; a ray of sunshine, and it was gone!

What! The ballot gave the majority - a large majority! - to the official candidatures, to the personal of the government, - and the *senatus consultum* increases the prerogatives of the Legislative Body! It therefore recognizes that the official candidates do not represent the public opinion!

And the Senate - the Senate, immortal gods! - will sanction that interpretation!

So the prefects did not have the happy hand! Their candidates, disoriented, are confronted with reforms that they had neither desired nor foreseen, and which they will accept, however. A painful situation, which recalls a formula of political economy: they will let do, the government let them pass!

A painful situation, let us repeat, since "the changes introduced into the constitutions of the empire" (Mr. Rouher's speech) concern only the relations between the great bodies of the State, doing not affect their prerogatives. They are the sophisticated tools, nothing more, entrusted to our deputies; and, when one thinks of their task: laws on the press, laws on meetings, and so on, one is not without anxiety; one hopes little of those workers of the last hour, that their natural vocation certainly did not designate for such a job. We shall see it, if they are not dismissed.

Without delay on the value of these modifications or largesse, I repeat my question: How do they meet the demands of the public opinion?

The opinion! Where to take it, where to seize it, where to find it? The booklets of grievances were presented in the language of the electorate - a language of equivocation and difficulties; - the Emperor, conforming himself to the spirit of the Constitution to retain in the accomplishment of the reforms to which had become necessary the appearance of initiative, the Emperor translated sovereignty and given *motu proprio* to the parliamentary guarantees contained in the *senatus consultum*.

How was this translation received?

Everything is saved! The country has what it asked, - the third party said.

Everything is compromised! The country asked for nothing, - the old majority replied.

All is lost! The country demanded another thing, - the left exclaimed.

What conclusions can be drawn from these contradictory assertions, from these various pretensions, from this solemn election, which means sometimes a reaction, sometimes a revolution, sometimes a peaceful progress? What conclusions can be drawn from this tumult, from this mess, from this chaos, except that an electoral system that, fit itself to such confusions, is essentially vicious?

The *double simultaneous vote*, the one I am proposing, the rational application of the *self-government*, only will be able to, under the present circumstances, without a special convocation, by force of circumstances, appoint a true constituent assembly, and before any meeting, before the opening of the session, from the very beginning of the vote, the classification of deputies, an easy and infallible operation, will have given the complete, precise and indisputable program of the reforms demanded by the country!

TRANSLATOR'S NOTE

District. In modern times, several politicians have presented proposals for improving the choice of representatives. One of them, not namely mentioned by Borély, was Deputy Condorcet, before fleeing in 1793, after having his arrest enacted by the group of Robespierre. He proposed in France a new voting system, in a single round, aimed at the correction of the old majority district voting system. In the old system, the elector chooses one among the several candidates presented and the candidate who obtains the highest number of votes in the circumscription wins. That electoral system is cheap and regionalized - it does not elects celebrities, - but it imbeds a great problem, recognized by all: it excludes the minorities, in practice, because the elector tends to choose between the candidate who represents the party of the situation and the one who has better chances of representing the oppositions. It is a system that, in its operation, has everything of bipartisan, although allows for the existence of many parties.

Method. The so-called *Condorcet Method* seeks to make room for more candidates and therefore more parties. Instead of just marking a name, the voter indicates his preferences. It does not mark an "X", but writes a number: 1, for first preference; 2, for second preference, and so on. For example, if there are four candidates, [ ] Andrews, [ ] Charles, [ ] Michael and [ ] Peter, representing four parties, the voter writes: [3] Andrews, [2] Charles, [1] Michael and [4] Peter. Adding the vote of all voters, the electoral judges give victory to those who reach the lesser number, which is the representation of the greater preference. If there is a tie, some previously agreed criteria is adopted, so that there is no impasse.

Quotient. The system proposed by Condorcet improves the old model a bit, but does not represent a rupture in front of it. And it is impractical when there are large numbers of candidates in the circumscription. Before this method, in 1780, Duke of Richmond proposed to the British Parliament a system in which the total number of voters of the country was divided by the 558 seats of the House of Commons, in order to obtain the number of voters to elect each representative. The project was rejected, but the idea of the electoral quotient was registered. So it is that in the book "Representative Government", of 1861, John Stuart Mill presents his appeal for the proportionality of the electoral representation. In 1869, Jules Borély, a Belgian teacher based in Paris, wrote the present book, presenting the mathematical formula that responds to this demand, and the work is published in 1870 (1).

Conditions. In order to the proportionality really to work, a fundamental requirement is cast for Borély upon the political system: every citizen needs to be literate. The reason for this is that voting must be compulsory for all people over "21-year-olds". It is not something that has been ignored in the application of the proposal. What is still under contempt, to date, is the component of the *simultaneous double vote*. In this system, the voter votes first in the party, the partisan vote being thus obligatory, which will form the proportion of the seats, and in the sequence is that the vote in the candidate, or candidates, is given, no matter if belonging to different party (2). A second round is not necessary, whereas the voting in each party is going to be allocated in the seats that the party obtained, observing the partisan vote given by the voter.

Halter. The exaggerated power of the electoral committees in the district system, denounced by Borély, shows its strength even today in countries that have not yet implemented the proportional voting. In early 2016, President Barack Obama defended obligatory voting, after being informed that in certain USA communities the electoral title is denied to people who do not seem favorable to the local leaders, just as it happened in Latin America in times of the coronelism and the "halter voting".

Nominal. In 1875 the book "La Democracia Práctica" (The Practical Democracy) was published in Paris, in Spanish, by the magistrate and deputy Luís Vicente Varela, an Argentine born in Uruguay, where his father, Florencio Varela, was exiled. In this book of 504 pages, dedicated to "the parliaments of the American republics", available today on the Internet, the author studies all electoral systems of the important countries of his time and review in depth the work of Borély. Among other things, he disagrees with the vote cast on several candidates and questions the claim that in the model presented there are no "lost votes". He also rejects the proportion by the partisan vote, and not by the name of the candidate, arguing that the voter is not ever a partisan, and this criticism continues to be respected, which leads to the "Tiririca" effect" (3).

Streams. In addition to making Borély's work accessible to the Iberian-speaking public, Varela gives the model a very valuable contribution, which is the proposal of the *sublems*. Borély could not predict that his method would bring the contrary problem to the restricted number of parties represented, of one or two: in the proportional model the trend is for the fragmentation, which, for governability, can be harmful. Thus, it is known today, the application of the proportional representation system requires strong measures against the participation of small parties. To the judge or legislator who fears the risk of one-party rule, Varela presents the adoption of the *sublems*. Suppose that only one or two parties remain in the country. Then they are officially divided into two or three streams, each one, for the purpose of a proportional dispute. Jose Marti published in Mexico a comment very favorable to the book of Varela. His country, Cuba, which in the beginning of the 21st century works under a single party, can calmly embrace Varela's proposal, dividing the official party into two or, preferably, three *sublems*, in order to finally implant the proportional vote in the country (this cannot be confused with the sub-stream system of majority elections, which the 1964 regime adopted in Brazil).

Barrier. The maximum number of parties that Borély takes into account is seven - he did not see the possibility of greater number, - the coalitions being totally forbidden. Of these seven, one was center, having on its left the left wing, center-left and extreme left, with conservative antipodes on the right. Now, there is the center-left and the center-right, but there is not, in practice, the center. Parliaments are usually divided in the middle by a corridor, with half of the seats on the left and another half on the right. So we can imagine that the ideal number of streams is six. But this number is still large, considering that extreme-left and extreme-right parties are anti-democratic - as experience has already shown, - and their representatives must be diluted in civilized parties. The number of the represented streams must therefore be four: left, center-left, center-right and right. In terms of colors, we can think of red, yellow, green and blue. Nevertheless, if we assume that the limit should be six, what exceeds this number has a great chance of being faction of extremists or herd led by opportunists.

Highlights. While seeing with current eyes the proposed system, the attention is drawn to at least five items: a) the proportion in the Chamber is by the partisan vote, with *simultaneous double vote*, in the party and in the candidate; b) the *obligatory* vote is intrinsic to the idea of proportional voting; c) the model requires the *prohibition of coalitions*; d) all citizens must be *literate*; e) number of parties greater than *seven* is not considered.

Ripening. Although Borély imagined that his formula, with all the justifications embedded, was easy and immediate to assimilate, this was not the case, since France, the country to which the study is devoted first, only adopted the proportional vote in March 1986 - 116 years after the publication of the book, - under the presidency of François Mitterrand. The accounts, in fact, are easy to understand; difficult is to perceive the advantages of the model.

(1) A little book of 2011, published in the Internet, analyzes the influence of Stuart Mill in France at that period ("The Reception of John Stuart Mill in France", Vincent. Guillin and Djamel Souafa).

(2) Anyway, Uruguay adopts this model since 1910.

(3) Parliamentarian Tiririca (Francisco Everardo), humorist of TV, obtained more than one million votes, dragging with him several candidates with scarce votes. One way to mitigate this kind of problem is to lead the voter to always vote for two candidates - not for several, like Borély wished, nor for one, like Varela advocated.

Cacildo Marques - translator

cacildomarques@gmail.com
@cacildo

Printed in Great Britain
by Amazon